Innovation
for
Underdogs

How to Make the Leap
From What If to Now What

Dr. David Pensak
with
Elizabeth Licorish

CAREER
PRESS
The Career Press, Inc.
Franklin Lakes, NJ

INNOVATION FOR UNDERDOGS
EDITED BY JODI BRANDON
TYPESET BY MICHAEL FITZGIBBON
Cover design by Howard Grossman/12e Design
Printed in the U.S.A. by Book-mart Press

To order this title, please call toll-free 1-800-CAREER-1 (NJ and Canada: 201-848-0310) to order using VISA or MasterCard, or for further information on books from Career Press.

CAREER PRESS

The Career Press, Inc., 3 Tice Road, PO Box 687,
Franklin Lakes, NJ 07417
www.careerpress.com

Library of Congress Cataloging-in-Publication Data

Pensak, David.
    Innovation for underdogs : how to make the leap from what if to now what / by David Pensak with Elizabeth Licorish
    p. cm.
    Includes index.
    ISBN 978-1-60163-035-3
    1. Technological innovations. 2. Change. I. Licorish, Elizabeth. II. Title.

HD45.P412 2008
658.4′063--dc22

2008034552

For my father, Louis Pensak

Contents

Foreword

Dr. David Pensak believes that we are all born curious and ready to innovate. As kids, he says, we do innovate and improvise to fulfill our boundless needs, dissatisfactions, and curiosities. As we become adults, however, our careers—and even our educations—stifle our innovative instincts. With *Innovation for Underdogs*, Dr. Pensak explains how would-be innovators can recapture the spirit of curiosity and creativity, how they can gain the initiative to become successful problem solvers. After all, innovators are great inquisitors; they are underdogs.

Dr. Pensak is an innovator who has had a tremendous impact on a grand scale. At the dawn of the Internet era, he anticipated the need to keep information-outsiders on the outside, and the firewall he ultimately created became the crux of present and future Internet security. He successfully launched a company around his groundbreaking idea and marketed his innovation to highly creative companies. Dr. Pensak's innovation insight is invaluable because it stems from solid experience.

David Pensak has an extremely precise understanding of the types of innovations and their functions in the world of business. He believes that successful innovations are rarely attributed to good luck. Dr. Pensak's critiques of famed and failed innovations are essential to both the amateur entrepreneur and the head of a well-established corporation. For three decades, Dr. Pensak played an indispensible role at one of the United States' most distinguished and successful enterprises, an innovative giant intent on improving millions of lives. Drawing upon his experiences, David Pensak assures company CEOs that their biggest assets are innovative employees. The pages of *Innovation for Underdogs* are filled with novel ways businesses can successfully motivate their workers by fostering their creative capacities. Dr. Pensak effectively inspires individuals at the bottom of the corporate ladder at the same time he instructs company CEOs.

Innovation for Underdogs presents every underdog with the opportunity to think like some of the world's most creative minds. David is both a skilled organic chemist and a shining computer scientist. Though few of us have such intellectual tools to work with, David teaches that successful innovation really stems from a mindset accessible to all. Identify needs and dissatisfactions in the marketplace and tap into your natural curiosities. Be on the lookout for unconventional solutions; take an idea from one walk of life and apply it to another. Think about how something is; then think about how it should be. To illustrate these points, David expertly explains how his greatest ideas have stemmed from the fundamentals of his day-to-day life.

Innovation is the driving force behind human progress. Creativity must be constantly pursued in order for a society to continually address the needs of its people. History shows us the devastating effects of not enough innovation; amazingly, third-century BC Rome and 17th-century England shared staggeringly similar levels of wealth. For 2,000 years, a serious lack of innovation deprived humanity of its essential need for growth. Unfortunately, this trend continues today. Many of today's developing countries are so under-innovative that several billion people are left to live hungry, sick, and hopeless. *Innovation for Underdogs* carefully examines promising new social innovations such as the Grameen Bank's micro-loan and the programs introduced by the Columbian Coffee Federation; at the same time, it calls for even more innovation in the Third World.

David Pensak has given extremely popular speeches on innovation in developing countries such as Brazil, Jordan, and Thailand; in the future he will teach innovation in such places as Sub-Saharan Africa and India. Whether he is speaking in Sao Paulo, Amman, or Bangkok, whether he is working out real innovative solutions or discussing hypothetical opportunities, it is a great treat to watch David teach some of the developing world's most talented, aspiring innovators how to identify their own marketplace needs, dissatisfactions, and curiosities. American managers might think that emerging countries are merely suppliers of cheap commodities and low-cost labor. David Pensak's work seriously challenges those who believe this to think again.

The world has never been better prepped for innovation. The Internet Age has made both research and communication significantly easier to achieve. Monopolies and state-owned enterprises are being forced to compete with burgeoning independent ventures. Trade and investment barriers are being toppled. New technologies are making it possible to establish businesses without massive capital and expansive organizational capacities. All that we need to access these opportunities is a little creativity and a new, uninhibited way of thinking. *Innovation for Underdogs* is a touching personal memoir about one of the world's greatest innovators, a collection of inspirational success stories, and an anecdotal guidebook for every underdog hoping to get ahead.

Michael P. Ryan, PhD
Director, Creative and Innovative Economy Center
The George Washington University Law School

Chapter 1

Who Needs Fire Hydrants? How the Underdog Innovates Firewalls

I've traveled around the globe, from Geneva to Amman to Bangkok and Sao Paulo, to speak to the minds of the world's most esteemed corporations and prestigious universities about innovation. A lot of the time, I'm shocked to see how insecure even the top brains of these organizations are about their own innovative abilities. There is a mysticism surrounding the concept of innovation that scares even the best of the best from even attempting to follow their dreams.

The misconception is that the ability to innovate is exclusive, magically bestowed upon some lucky few who alone hold the power to change the world. But the mind-power behind innovation is quite basic, extremely logical, and certainly inherent in any human being living and breathing today. It's scary to realize that, all too often, the big guys in charge think it is much easier to intimidate than to innovate. These same business executives and academic scholars won't believe in their own powers of innovation because they don't want to believe in the creative capacities of their subordinates.

These little guys are the underdogs, the men and women of the world who have been trained against their nature to believe that the answer is always no. Throughout human history, underdogs have been habitually brainwashed to believe that being able to innovate requires a huge amount of specialized intellect, the power of status, and the privilege of wealth. Even if your average Joe let's himself dream of innovation for even a second, he's likely to think he needs an education in astrophysics before he could ever be creative. Yet if you asked the same guy to name one of the best innovations of all time, he would probably tell you he couldn't imagine a world without something as simple as sliced bread. Very few innovations involve exclusively specialized knowledge; even those that do don't start out with complicated formulas, charts, and graphs. They all start out with discovering a problem.

My students ask me all the time to tell them how I created the Internet firewall, and I tell them, first and foremost, that the story isn't about how I *created* Raptor Systems; it is about how I discovered the need for it. Raptor didn't result from a desire to make a ton of money, or to dazzle the world with new technology, or even to fulfill an imminent call for Internet security. I created the first commercially successful Internet firewall only because I wanted to help a friend.

Innovation stems from three things: needs, dissatisfactions, and curiosities. A friend of mine had a great need when a manipulated business deal almost ruined his life. He was the president of the U.S. subsidiary of a

British computer company, enjoying quite a lucrative position and a much-more-than-comfortable life with his wife and his children in their beautiful home. He'd been in the business of making money off of computer hardware his entire career, so when his company presented him with the opportunity to buy a large quantity of computer hardware with the promise of making a huge profit, he bought it right up and thanked his privilege as president for the deal.

It wasn't until he'd invested everything he had and mortgaged his house that the company announced a new model of hardware that was twice the speed and half the price of the stuff he'd just bought with his entire life. All of a sudden, there seemed to be absolutely no way for him to market the hardware in the face of such superior competition. He was devastated and scared to death that the failure would surely mean losing his house and ruining his family. For a while, I didn't think I could do anything to help.

The two of us were in a New York City taxicab heading to a meeting one day at precisely the same time my friend's situation looked as though it would wreck him forever. He told me it was almost certain he would lose his house and that his wife would leave him and take his kids. He was terrified of losing everything he had except the huge quantity of undesirable computer hardware that couldn't pay for a cup of coffee, much less his home mortgage or his children's college tuitions. Finally he looked at me with tears in his eyes, and he was shaking when he said, "My whole family is at stake here, David; what can we do?"

I knew there was no way we were going to sell the hardware as it was, but there is something about envisioning your dear friend homeless and living in a box that forces you to think outside of it. So as we rode along the city streets, I pondered the idea between potholes until finally I said, "Well, the only thing that comes to mind is to come up with some software that can be sold only with the hardware in your inventory. We have to generate software that is so incredibly valuable that people won't care how much they have to pay for the hardware it runs on."

After I thought about it some more, I figured that what people consider most valuable is something they all hold in common: the desire to protect their assets. It turned out that protecting my friend's assets by helping him avoid bankruptcy meant innovating a way for all people to protect their worth where it is most at stake: the Internet.

All this was happening in the early 1990s, during the time when people were still reveling in the newness and the fantastic potential of the Internet, so much so that they hadn't really considered just how vulnerable the Internet left individual people and entire organizations. Even DuPont, one of the most innovative institutions in the nation (where I had been doing computational chemistry), was not focused on developing protective programming at that time.

Yet, when I considered the problem I was trying to solve, coming up with some sort of security software was the perfect way to market the hardware by attaching it to a new and extremely important innovation. It didn't matter that my superiors hadn't thought up a similar idea first. It didn't even matter that I would have to use technology someone else invented to bring my innovation to life. Innovating something even as complex as a firewall never came down to answering every last intricate question about the technicalities surrounding the security of Internet information transmission. It came down to the fact that I had a problem: too much useless material belonging to too good a friend to be destroyed by debt. No one ever said to me, "Hey, David, can you come up with a way to encapsulate Internet data to assure its protection?" All anyone ever said was, "Hey, David, would you help me out?"

◈ ◈

The beauty of innovation is that it comes about in situations all people experience in life—in my case, innovation found me when I needed to help a friend. Innovation doesn't have to happen in a laboratory, during a "eureka" moment in which a mad scientist discovers some radioactive compound. In fact, such moments aren't examples of innovation at all.

When people *discover* something they weren't aware of before, they are actually inventing, not innovating. Innovation means taking existing technologies and processes and applying them to make a meaningful, measurable, and identifiable change in the way something is done. And the first step of innovation isn't discovering the solution, it's discovering the problem, usually a problem that any person can appreciate (such as financial ruin.) My Internet firewall innovation wasn't conjured up in a science lab; rather, it was conceived of commonly in the back seat of a New York City taxicab.

After I consummated my relationship with Internet security, I opened up my basement to a couple of friends and numerous pizzas and many half-gallon bottles of Coke in order to come up with a way to apply what we all already knew to the new problem we were trying to solve. Together we came up with a piece of software that inspired the kind of computer safety on which the world is entirely dependent today. It was an innovation that was technologically revolutionary for its time; yet, essentially, Raptor Systems was most inspired by exactly what it's named after: ordinary birds of prey.

I don't like people who break into computers. When the idea to create Internet security software first popped into my head, I didn't first think about how I'd manipulate technology to get the job done. Instead, I immediately thought about a cartoon I'd seen in the comics years before. It showed a buzzard sitting on a branch while looking massively irritated and extremely hungry in the empty desert. The caption at the bottom read, "Patience, Hell, I'm gonna kill the first thing that moves!" That kind of fearless predatory conviction is what I wanted my software to model; I wanted a program that would systematically and flawlessly eliminate any foreign and suspicious data from going into or coming out of any computer system. And because, at the time, nothing in the world could do this, I had to take my inspiration from birds instead of computer programming.

There is a family of birds called raptors that subsists solely by eating live prey. The eagle is the most well known of these birds, so I proposed to name my software in its honor: Raptor Eagle. Similarly, I named the company I assembled to create the product Raptor Systems. I thought I had hit my stride when it came to giving clever names to business and merchandise, and so I single-handedly decided to select the company motto, too: "We'll catch 'em; you get to kill 'em." Needless to say, it was catchy, but it didn't catch on, and I found out the hard way that even successful innovators have their limits; I would never have a future in sales or marketing.

I didn't take my inspiration entirely from birds. In creating the Raptor firewall, I learned a little bit along the way from frogs, too. I once read an extremely fascinating article: "What the Frog's Eye Tells the Frog's Brain," which says a lot for science. Frogs, obviously, are not organisms of extremely high intellect. Most people learn this in high school science. Remember the lesson in which dropping a frog in boiling water prompts him to immediately jump out of the pot, while dropping him into lukewarm water and slowing bringing the heat to high will cause the same little Kermit to be cooked to death? Frogs recognize things by instinct, not cognitive process. When a frog kills a fly it isn't because the fly looks tasty; it's because the frog's vision only allows him to see organisms that move at the specific speed and with the precise motions of a fly.

Of course, I couldn't create software that would destroy everything that "moves" on a computer. I needed a piece of programming that would selectively target data that moves in a suspicious or unfamiliar way, just as a frog recognizes a fly. The program's features would included suspicious activity detection, contrived to help system managers moderate what was going on in a network. If a file, normally accessed three to four times a week, suddenly started being accessed a hundred times a day, the Raptor system would take notice and set itself up for the kill. Innovating is about applying existing technologies and processes to make meaningful change in the way something is done. In this case, I just took the way the frog kills a fly and applied it to computers to change the way they handle dangerous data.

As long as I provided the beer, the Coke, and the pizza, and as long as all the members of the Raptor crew got their fair shares of stock in the company, they were very happy to work with me on nights and weekends to develop new systems. We devised another product called the Hawk that shared some functions with the Eagle, and even subdivisions of the Eagle called Eaglets, which detected suspicious activity separately in different departments of a computer system.

We devised a system that processed information similar to the way a secretary would when it comes to processing information. I was very excited when I discovered that there is indeed a bird called the secretary bird. It lives in Africa, and it runs with feathers sticking out on the sides of its head, so that it resembles the prototypical Lily Tomlin secretary with a pencil over her ear in the movie *9 to 5*. I wish I could have used this discovery to brilliantly name our then latest creation, but my colleagues convinced me there was no way we could go into any corporate office and sell a product called the Secretary Bird. I understood their point, although I still retain a belief in how nice it would be if secretaries could act as firewalls, too. Taking care of secretarial and security procedures at the same time would be a brilliantly innovative way to kill two birds with one stone.

❧ ❧

When I talk to students and professionals about my firewall, I tell them that it's not important to understand the painful details about how the software operates. As a future innovator, the most important thing to observe about my innovation is what it operates *like*. Again, innovation means applying the way something already exists or operates to a new field, product, or process in order to make a meaningful change. It's about drawing observations from what you already know works, and applying them to what you want to make work for the very first time. Understanding why the firewall is so important is more similar to understanding the significance of the telephone or the postal service than understanding the intricacies of computer technology. Don't believe me? I'll show you.

Back when the rocks were soft and you wanted to place a telephone call, you would simply pick up the phone and the operator would say, "Number please." Then you'd simply give her the number and she would plug it in and connect you. This worked fine for a while, but the extrapolation in the 1940s was that if everyone in the United States wound up having a telephone, one third of all American adults would have to be telephone operators. That's why the phone companies developed the electronic switching systems, and dial tones, and all the other wonderful innovations that keep one-on-one communication possible to people across the globe.

Today, people communicate primarily over the Internet, which does not involve direct point-to-point communication the way telephones do. This is because the Internet is one great big network. If I talk to a colleague on the phone, I can feel fairly secure because the phone company sets up a direct line between just the two of us. But if I e-mail a colleague over the Internet, it isn't possible to isolate our two computers and connect them directly to each other. Internet e-mail depends on what are called "store and forward computers." When I send e-mail, each block of a message is stored on one computer and then sent out to a second computer; then the second computer determines whether or not it has gotten the message without any errors. Once this happens, the first computer deletes the message and the second sends it on to a third computer.

The problem with this is that an Internet e-mail sequence can end up resembling the elementary-school game "whisper down the lane"; the correct message can end up being retained on the wrong computer in the chain. For instance, most people have had the experience of sending an e-mail and receiving a message back that says something along the lines of, "Sorry, we couldn't deliver your message; don't resend it, and we'll get back to you." Sometimes, for whatever reason, one computer in a chain will not be up during the time you send an e-mail. When this happens, the message gets stored on a computer in the chain for some indeterminable period of time. As long as your message is sitting on another computer (and a lot of these store-and-forward computers are at universities), there is always an opportunity for people to tap in to your message.

⊀ ⊁

Working at DuPont, I was extremely aware of just how important maintaining confidentiality is, especially over the Internet. If a company e-mail were to get stuck on some unaffiliated computer, it would be exceptionally likely that someone—anyone—could access it on the server and say to himself or herself, "Gee, there's an e-mail from DuPont to The National Institute for Health. I wonder what I will find inside that might help me in the stock market."

The worst part about having information stolen over the Internet is that you're not likely to know that you've been ripped off. Stealing an Internet message is not comparable to stealing a book. When you steal a book, the person notices it's gone, but when you make a copy of a message on your computer, the person you've stolen from still has his original copy, and he doesn't know that he's been robbed. The biggest contribution I made to the world of Internet security was devising a way to encapsulate information so that there was a way to detect any interference a message experienced en route from sender to receiver. And because innovation is about thinking outside the box, I looked out at the world around me to see if any system in existence could be applied to what I was trying to do with the Internet. In looking at the world around me, I discovered the power of envelopes, and so, I sat down with my company to model an Internet safety device that resembled the workings of the European post.

If you order a package through the mail and it arrives at your doorstep half-opened, you might have good cause to take issue with your mailman. Envelopes aren't easily tampered with discreetly; many a child has tried to open and forge a report card, only to have his efforts given away by the impossibility of effectively re-securing the sticky seal. Considering this, it makes perfect sense that confidential company e-mails, which surely are more important to conceal than the grade point average of a fifth grader, should be placed in computerized envelopes that can show if they have been interrupted by an unwelcome third party. Thus, Raptor Systems set out to make e-mail just as secure as the snail-mail variety.

In the United States, there are literally hundreds of sizes of envelopes people can mail their packages in, depending on the size of the items they want to ship. Any size envelope, from 2×3 to 18×24, can be processed by the U.S. postal system; they're all legal. But in most European countries, people may use only four of five different-sized envelopes, because it is easier to impose safety regulations on a limited selection of sizes. I decided that, due to the vast quantity of critical information the Internet ships every day, my security software needed to one-up even the European postal service when it came to standardizing the size envelope in which information could be packaged. In order for messages to be sent via e-mail securely, I needed to create a one-size-fits-all "virtual wrapping paper" that would encapsulate any size and type of message, from a small friendly greeting to a large business contract, and secure it from any and all prying eyes.

❧ ❧

Innovation means taking existing technologies and processes, and applying them to make a meaningful, measurable, and identifiable change in the way something is done. Innovating the first Internet firewall sounds extremely complex to the average human being, but really, the vast majority of this particular innovation is due, in large part, to understanding processes as simple as mailing a letter. A large part of developing Raptor Systems involved researching the achievements of the early founders of the Internet. I knew that my software wasn't going to reinvent the wheel; to innovate Internet security, I only had to consider the parts people had already built, and put them together for a new purpose. I share the story behind Raptor Systems time and time again, not because it is an extraordinary example of how innovation works, but because it illustrates how even the most seemingly complex innovations can be reduced to the task of finding a problem and looking to the world outside the scenario for a solution.

Through the years I've spent teaching and lecturing on innovation around the world, I've harvested quite a collection of remarkable stories. Throughout this book, I'll share with you how some of the world's greatest innovations were conceived. I'll give you the advent of creations ranging from innovations in the computer and medical industries to innovations in pizza and sex. No matter the innovation, each success involves the same process, the same style of thinking, and the same way of life—a life that finds opportunity in needs, dissatisfactions, and curiosities. It is a way of life that's accessible to all, especially those on the bottom rung of life's ladder. I've never met anyone more in need, more dissatisfied, or more curious than an underdog.

Chapter 2

The Inquisitive Underdog Gets the Bone: How Simple Questions Yield Astronomical Answers

Any person who has ever dreamed of finding a landmark solution to any problem must first learn how to ask questions. I am writing this book, as a whole, in honor of my father, Louis Pensak, an incredible innovator and revolutionary thinker. My dad made waves all across the seas of science, from the laboratories of Nobel Prize–winning physicists to the great legacy of Einstein himself. But what made my father such a masterful innovator was the way he never lost the spirit of the underdog, the humble inquisitiveness and innocent open-mindedness that allowed him to relate to and encourage the smallest child as well as the most renowned scientist.

My father's legacy was the way he taught his colleagues and me so much, so gently, about "thinking about thinking." It was this that he titled the book he was writing when he died. He was 150 pages through it, and I sure wish he had been able to innovate a better way to handwrite so that I could make out all his words. But, in a sense, I don't have to. His legacy lives through me, and I hope that, with this book, it will live through you, too.

For all of his achievements, my father was born very humbly in Brooklyn, New York, in 1912. His father owned a leather goods store and ran a booming business until the Depression hit in the 1930s. Ever faithful to his employees, my grandfather went bankrupt paying his staff out of pocket when work income wasn't enough to suffice company salaries. But my father didn't want to learn to operate sewing machines for pennies to his name; instead he decided to study physics.

Needless to say, the family was quite upset to see my dad leave for the world of academia, a seemingly less practical solution to the problems of paucity. Nevertheless, my father succeeded magnificently in his education at Long Island University; he thrived in a career dedicated to innovative science, and, in the process, helped change the way the world thinks about solving its greatest problems.

When he passed away in 1970, my father had more than 80 patents to his name, and he had long been hailed as one of the world's most significant contributors to the field of electrical engineering. His work made possible some of humankind's most important innovations, such as Jack Kilby's transistor and the device used to analyze the anatomy of Einstein's brain. My father was even a leading mentor to Herbert Kroemer, the scientist who won the 2000 Nobel Prize in Physics for developing semiconductor heterostructures used in high-speed and opto-electronics.

All his life, my father was able to generate countless answers to endless problems, and, furthermore, he inspired solutions in everyone around him. I am so very fortunate to have been surrounded by such achievement in my youth. But for all of his complex and elegant answers, my father always kept his focus on asking questions and opening up his mind in the fashion of a curious child. And so it was the problems my father embraced, not necessarily his revolutionary answers, that made him such a role model to me. His was a role and a purpose that anyone can fulfill.

❧ ❧

Every child is a born innovator because every child looks at the world in wonderment. Children are so naturally inclined to ask questions about everything they see, but too often the adults of the world are reluctant to provide them with answers. This happens for a lot of different reasons. For instance, "Mom, where do babies come from?" is a question often squelched for the sake of protecting a child from knowledge that adults think should be handled with more maturity. Not in my house.

When I was in kindergarten, I was absolutely mesmerized by a classroom experiment in egg incubation. Watching our eggs, inanimate and generally uninteresting for weeks, turn into the most adorable and plush little lives in front of my face genuinely moved my 6-year-old soul. It should be easy to imagine the terror I felt when I realized the origin of my mother's omelets over breakfast the next morning; I was absolutely horrified to see cracked shells lying empty and violated next to the sizzling pan of yellow about to land on my plate. I found myself in a fit of hysterics over that meal; I immediately ran over to my mother and pleaded with her not to kill the baby chickens, to just give me cereal instead. My mother and father were obviously startled by my panic, but instead of hushing my objection to breakfast, they sat me down and invited me to tell them every-thing I knew (and everything I didn't.)

All of this happened so long ago, but I clearly re-member this conversation as one of the greatest mo-ments of learning in my life. Mom and Dad spent the better part of an hour explaining to me the birds and the bees (poultry version), and informing me gently that the eggs I'd been eating for breakfast every morning were not the same as the ones I had seen hatch into little chicks in class. My father's uncle had a small chicken farm in Lakewood, New Jersey, so my folks even took me up there so that I could see chickens in all stages of development and ask more questions about how they were taken care of.

After the farm trip, I was able to eat breakfast with a much improved level of composure. My parents must have been reasonably pleased with their efforts until a few months later, when my particular panic about egg ethics turned into a very large concern with all animal gestation. For the next year or two, Mom and Dad must have been convinced that their chicken talk had un-leashed a mini monster.

The number of questions I asked about where "ba-bies" of different species came from almost convinced my parents they had unwittingly guaranteed my future as an obstetrician. It became a worry that I was slowly losing my mind when one of my guppies had about 20 little babies and I insisted on giving each its own unique name. I couldn't understand why my little brother was not able to recognize each one from the others at the same time my parents were probably coming to terms with their crazy child.

Eventually, as most children eventually do, I learned a little bit about what separates animals from humans. (Although, today, my six bichon frises are most certainly

a huge part of my family.) But, having had these experiences, I came out of childhood ahead of the game: I was
equipped with valuable knowledge about the nature of
life and the world. I'd learned that things are often not
what they seem; that seemingly identical objects likely
have completely different purposes.

As a child, I learned, quite memorably, that eggs
can create life on a farm at the same time they can contribute energy to the human body. As an adult, I would
use this model to relate the postal service to Internet
security and come up with a landmark innovation. I
was able to do this because my parents allowed me to
ask questions—as many as I needed, as long as some
kind of solution seemed possible. (My parents, in fact,
would commonly ask, "Is that your final answer?" long
before Regis Philbin did.)

❧ ❧

Sometimes, adults don't answer children's questions
because they think the answers are too complex for
young minds; more often, though, the correct answers
are even too complex for the parents. For example, a
child curious about how a car runs or how e-mail works
is often discouraged form asking such questions because,
most of the time, Mom or Dad just doesn't know the answer. But parents and teachers don't necessarily have
to know all of the answers for which children are searching;
the best questions don't always have obvious solutions.
The first secret to raising a world full of creative thinkers is learning how to let young people know that asking
questions and detecting problems is just as important as
finding answers.

Kids ask questions, incessantly it seems, to the tired
and frazzled parent, but the solution to this situation isn't
to say, "Not now" or "We'll talk about it later." Children

don't ask so many questions because they are spontaneously compelled to by nature; they are so curious because they usually never receive enough information to occupy their minds beyond their original thoughts. When a child asks a question that seems completely irrelevant to the question he or she asked just seconds before, it's as though he or she is really saying, "Okay, that was a bad question because it doesn't have an answer; how about this one?" Many parents think themselves anxious to put a stop to their children's continuous streams of questions. In reality though, the stress lives in the children, who are desperate for direction.

When I was growing up, I knew it was okay to ask questions. Growing up with my father and his colleagues, I was always surrounded by questions, such as "How do we do this?" or "How is this happening?" or "Is there any way we can make this happen?" (and "If we can make this happen, what else can we do?"). Sometimes, my inquisitiveness would get me in trouble in school, where my teachers were often taken aback by my knack for answering their questions with other questions.

When I was in second grade, my teacher, Miss Coderre, assigned each student a book report. I had never put together such an ensemble, so I asked Miss Coderre what she wanted us to do with the assignment. She answered that this was an excellent question, and told the class to pay very careful attention as she wrote "who, what, when, where, why" on the blackboard. This seemed simple enough, and I was very pleased at how easily I was able to answer these five questions so concisely (it seemed) in the pages of my report. When I got the assignment back a week later, I felt as sick as I did when I imagined my mother slaughtering baby chickens in her frying pan: I'd received a failing grade.

I was raised to ask questions if and whenever any aspect of the world around me didn't make sense. And so I had no hesitation to walk right up to the front of the room and demand Miss Coderre explain why she had given me such a low grade for answering everything she had asked for. I remember she was stunned to get such an articulate pushback from a 6-year-old, but she stopped what she was doing and formulated a great answer: "You answered the five "W" questions, but you never wrote about what you learned from the book and how it will help you grow into a stronger and smarter adult." This surprised me, but it didn't leave me satisfied, and so I replied back to Miss Coderre, "How will I know when I have done that?"

Being a very sincere and dedicated teacher, Miss Coderre was too worried she had been misdirecting her class to fret that the issue had been raised by one of her small students. By asking the standard teacher questions, the five worthless W's, she had been leading the class down the slippery slope of learning by regurgitation instead of creativity and critical thinking. Miss Coderre had given me a low grade for doing what she had asked, without realizing that the problems with my report were with her questions and not my answers. By letting me raise questions of my own, she was able to find a way to steer the entire class toward a whole new perspective on learning.

Within seconds of hearing my concerns, she exclaimed to the whole class, "Let's read a book together and use the story to explore questions that have no right or wrong answers." Because of this, the entire class was able to delve into the riches of childhood literature with an enthusiasm that searches hungrily for the best questions and the most creative answers. All of our book reports turned out to be huge successes. I ran into Miss Coderre about 20 years ago, and she had a huge smile when she told me, "I learned a lot from you that day; it's too easy for adults to think that, because they are older, the best way to teach children is to reward repetition. Ever since I taught you, I've learned to teach children to think for themselves. Thank you."

❧ ❦

My father taught me that questions are journeys and explorations, not simply inquiries. Throughout elementary school, high school, and even college, children are confronted with questions intended only to gauge what they have memorized from their teachers' lectures and their textbooks' lessons. In this case, teachers are not asking questions; they are dealing students prompts: "According to our study guide, what are the most prominent stages of human evolution?" When a teacher or a parent asks a child a question, the issue should not have an answer neatly typed out in a textbook, a study guide, or a bible. Relating back to a lesson on evolution, a real question, such as "How does human evolution relate to other processes of nature?" might only be answered by first asking another questions, such as "What problems have others detected with classification systems?" or "What exactly is a process of nature?"

Learning how to innovate, whether you are an adult or a child, means learning (or relearning) that some questions make great answers. "Why is the sky blue?" is a question that is best explored by asking other questions such as "What makes blue different than green?" or "Why is the sky sometimes gray?" Questions and answers do not make up one-way streets; they make up a whole playground of discovery and curiosity that requires a child's state of mind, no matter how complex the material, to reach. Questions are about pushing back boundaries. Questions and answers are to innovators as chickens and eggs are to theorists and philosophers: once you are fully engaged in your thoughts and have opened yourself up to all possibilities, questions become answers and answers become questions, and, all the while, a ton of prospects pop up.

When I was about 10 years old, my little brother was born, and boy did he seem to love to scream all morning, mid-afternoon, late evening, and, most fervently, in the very darkest hour of the middle of the night. No matter the time of day, Martin was always shrieking his tiny head off despite how dry his diaper or how full his belly was. This was obviously a problem for my mother, who was growing weary from many a late-night scream fest, for my father, whose work left him unable to routinely comfort a wailing infant, and for me, as I found myself wondering about adoption. In finding the solution to the upset baby problem, my father didn't just ask himself, "How do I get little Martin to be quiet?" On top of this question, he asked himself, "*Why* is little Martin crying?" Then, he assigned me as the detective to figure out the mystery behind the mayhem.

While my parents salvaged time together over morning coffee, it was my job to sit with Martin and take notes on his behavior. We had already tried soothing Martin's screams by getting rid of everything he didn't like, such as soggy diapers and hunger pains. So instead of asking me to find out what Martin didn't like, my Dad assigned me to the task of figuring out what Martin *did* like. It turned out that Martin had a real taste for the element of surprise.

I got pretty desperate in my search for the solution to my younger brother's cries. For days I tried different things to calm him down. I would sing and dance around to different songs, and wave all sorts of objects from calculators to underwear in his face to try and amuse him.

One day, while Martin was crying, I started flipping the power button on my shiny new flashlight in what I thought was a pretty pathetic attempt to call him to some sort of order. I was surely surprised to discover that Martin was so fascinated by the changing light that the activity immediately hushed him.

My dad was thrilled with my discovery, but he gently let me know that, though I was making progress in solving the mystery, I wasn't necessarily done asking questions. What about the flashlight made our baby stop crying? Was it the light? Was it the dark after the light? Was it just the movement that the changing light seemed to simulate?

As we ran through some possible theories about why Martin so loved the flashlight, we discovered that Martin cried because he hated to be bored. Martin would stop crying when we started flicking the flashlight, but he would start to cry again the minute he recognized a pattern in the change of light. Yet when we flipped the switch on and off at random intervals, Martin found himself joyfully lost in the task of predicting what would happen to the light next.

Dad came up with the idea to design a board mounted with four flashlights, wired together in a network that would work to light each of the flashlights up in varied and unpredictable order. Of course, I was still just a child, so I wasn't able to handle the technology part of the endeavor myself, but my father made it clear to me that I had achieved the most important part of the discovery: using everything available to solve the problem, no matter how crazy a possible solution seemed, and no matter how many questions I needed to ask. Sure, Dad could put together the flashlight toy that would keep my brother amazed and silent for hours. But the baby would still be crying if someone hadn't done the real work of discovering whether or not a toy would calm Martin down, and, if so, what kind of toy that would be. And that someone was me.

⊰ ⊱

It might be tempting to think that a man such as my father, who raised his children to think creatively and adore all sorts of experiments, would harbor much disdain for electronic pleasures such as television. But this was absolutely not the case. My family owned one of the first televisions in the country and had been watching it for years even before I was born. After all, my father was one of television's early designers.

My father assembled the unit we had in our home from parts. The entire structure was about as big as a full-sized refrigerator, although its screen was just a mere 3 inches in diameter. Nevertheless, Dad was proud of the device, and my brothers and I adored it. So did our neighbors. Dad set up our television (the only one on the block) at the bottom of our basement steps, and, within hours our neighbors began the tradition of sitting on their cellar steps with binoculars to watch the magic illuminated on our makeshift TV screen.

I loved just about anything I could get on our television. In the early days, there were just three channels, but there was always something great to watch. A few years later, as televisions popped up in more and more homes across the country, there were 13 channels on which there was *usually* something good to watch. Today, there are hundreds of channels to choose from, yet it seems that there is virtually *never* anything worth watching.

Hence, television has gotten a bad rap as mindless, base-level entertainment that should be abandoned at all cost for more "intellectually stimulating" activities such as reading, writing, or playing around with math. This is because the value and the greatest purpose of television were forgotten long ago. Television can actually be one of the mind's greatest stimulators, and children and adults alike can do wonders for their innovative capacities just by sitting in front of the tube.

When I was a boy, my favorite TV show was *Atom Squad*, a daily science fiction program that captivated me from 5:00 to 5:15 every evening since its first airing in 1953. The "Atom Squad" was supposed to be the U.S. government's top-secret, high-tech defense team, which saved the world from various Cold War dangers such as nuclear bombs and radiation every night without fail. The Atom Squad did its most important work in the outer limits of space, using rockets and flying saucers, but the adventure of each show was so logical and well thought out that the program was entirely believable.

One evening, as I was watching a particularly exciting episode of *Atom Squad*, Dad's home-brew device malfunctioned and the tiny screen went off. I was too enchanted by the show to allow Dad to turn off the TV and troubleshoot the problem, so I just listened, riveted, to the sound. In this particular episode, the evildoers were employing some special metal-eating rotifers to threaten the security of the United States. The only way for the heroes to capture the villains was to build an entire submarine out of plastic to destroy the rotifers without being eaten. I had been following the show wonderfully until the screen blanked; the evil rotifers were not to be revealed until the end of the show, and so I felt very deprived that the rotifers, whatever they were, would remain mysterious to me forever. I had no idea what a rotifer was, or why such a thing could eat solid metal and not flimsy plastic.

My father saw I was frustrated, so he sat me down at the kitchen table after I listened to what I thought was the most disappointing *Atom Squad* ending ever. Dad brought out a pad of paper and a pencil, and he asked me to draw for him a picture of a rotifer. At this I felt more than a little chastised; Dad knew that the television had broken at the most important part of the show, so I couldn't imagine how he expected me to draw concepts I had never known and things I had never seen before.

I sat in my seat, stumped and irritated for a few minutes before my dad gently reminded me that metal-eating rotifers don't really exist, and that the people working on the *Atom Squad* show had to come up with the idea without looking at anything either. More importantly, he said, the Atom Squad's members had to come up with a way to outsmart what they had never seen before either; they had to imagine what the rotifers could be before they had to find and destroy them. Dad taught me then and there that no one can ever save the world the way the Atom Squad did without coming up with his or her own mental models, whether that person is fighting metal-eating rotifers, creating a television, or curing cancer.

✷ ✷

Television played a major role in how I grew up to be an innovator; it encouraged me to fantasize about everything I saw on screen and to believe in how my own imagination could transform or improve upon what somewhat else's mind had already created. Getting lost in a child's television show and letting yourself wonder "what if?" is exactly what it's like to open yourself up to the world of creativity and let your mind loose until it comes back with something otherworldly and innovative.

Anyone who has ever been an inquisitive child is purebred for innovation. It's a terrible reality, though, that too many children are stifled when they ask too many questions, just as curious dogs are fenced in and prohibited from exploring the world. Before anyone can learn from any of the world's greatest innovators, he or she must first learn how to think like children, who ask many questions and imagine a world of possibility inside their own minds. Being a great innovator means being a great inquisitor, a great underdog. I was lucky, because my father was both.

Chapter 3

Innovative Lessons From Einstein: How One Underdog Learned From the Masters

Here is the bottom line when it comes to training your mind to be innovative, whether you are a child or an adult: Innovation isn't accomplished by trying to stretch the brain into far-off realms of complex mathematics and science. Creative thought processes and innovative solutions are achieved by allowing the brain to relax into what it was designed to do, what it was allowed to do through childhood, yet ripped away from in adulthood. Innovation doesn't require fancy, grownup degrees, or prestigious positions at prominent companies. It calls simply for innovators to think like children.

I owe the whole of my innovative success to my childhood, a world where I was surrounded by brilliant innovators who taught me to think creatively as far back as before I even took my first steps. I grew up in a community that was filled with scientists and professors, because the bulk of my father's work involved designing the first television for RCA.

In the mid 1940s, RCA determined to move its research laboratories from New York City to Princeton, New Jersey. During this time, there was a nationwide shortage of housing, so RCA's employees were hard pressed to find places to live and raise their families. In order to solve this problem, the group of scientists collaborated to buy a large farm so that they could subdivide the land and build individual houses to fit each person's specifications. They didn't advertise the living arrangement, but soon enough word of mouth attracted even more and more of their colleagues, so that, eventually, RCA workers had created a unique and one-of-a-kind high-tech neighborhood.

A lot of people would probably assume that anyone who grew up surrounded by intellectuals would certainly grow up to be successful in some sort of technological or scientific field. But the truth of the matter is that it wasn't the fact that my mentors were intellectual that made me become an innovator myself; rather, it was what actually made them *successfully* intellectual that jump-started my own life of innovative achievement. The people who shaped my future did so because they possessed qualities that are accessible to anyone. Of course, they taught me how to ask questions. They also taught me to be appreciative, to realize the significance of little things, and to learn that something doesn't need to be visible to exist. From each creative adult I grew up with, I learned a wealth of very simple yet crucial points about innovation. These are the key facts about creativity that shaped my life so much that I want to share them in order help to shape yours.

When I was little, my father took me on a car trip from our home in Princeton to Davidson College in North

Carolina. Like any son sharing the road with his old man, I was thrilled to be seeing new sights, and I was caught up in the experience of the wide-open road. There is a certain sense of freedom that comes with fresh air as it smacks your face and wind as it whips your hair; and for all I know, it was moments such as these that primed my soul to embrace the innovative spirit. Yet, for all the adventure in the journey, there was all the more reward in the destination.

On this trip, my father journeyed back to see one of his old professors so that he could thank him for the wisdom he had shared and the intelligence he had fostered. He didn't bring me along for just any reason at all. One of my father's greatest endowments to my life was the way he taught me to think creatively, to innovate. But learning how to innovate is not an independently learned lesson.

❧ ❧

It is a mistake to believe that innovation means isolating your thoughts from others' successes in an attempt to be original or out-of-the-box. Innovation requires great regard and respect for what has come before, a kind of, what I like to call, "intellectual gratitude." Innovation is not invention, which is the discovery of something completely new; innovations make new out of what already exists, and so showing appreciation for the creative world of the past allows you to see the value it has for the future. Every flower has its root in history, and so earning praise as an innovator means first praising the past. If I, for instance, refused to acknowledge the technology that already existed in the realm of computers before I tackled innovating a firewall, I would never have had success with Raptor Systems.

The ability to innovate was handed down to me by my father as equally as it was taught to me by his colleagues. One of these men was none other than Albert Einstein, who lived his entire life in my hometown. When I was young, Einstein worked at the Institute for Advanced Study at Princeton University, which is where he stayed until he died in 1955. Living and working in the same area, he got to know my father and the other scientists at RCA quite well while he was alive. My father got to know Einstein even better after his death; he and his friend, pathologist Tom Harvey, designed the specialized equipment that analyzed Einstein's posthumous brain.

As a toddler, I used to love to sit on Mr. Einstein's lap, as I was apparently very fascinated by his wild head of hair. I remember that he spoke with accented speech I could then only identify as "different," but his language was rhythmic and engaging, and from the minute he'd open his mouth I would be at immediate attention. He was very good with the children in the community, and I have little doubt that his high achievement correlated quite closely with his enjoyment of the child like mind.

Einstein and his colleagues never stopped asking questions; they would ask me what I call "why" questions all of the time in order to challenge my beliefs and the lessons I learned in school. As a boy, I never had access to the specific genius behind his elegant and complex innovations, but I didn't need to; reinforcing my inquisitive nature was all the man had to do so that, later in life, I could come up with some important innovations of my own.

My father and Mr. Harvey, however, were insatiably curious about Einstein's genius. Mr. Harvey was the pathologist who performed the autopsy on Einstein's brain, and my father helped him design the equipment he needed for this special task. Shortly after he began studying the tissue more closely, my father would bring me to Mr. Harvey's lab and let me watch as they tried to determine the physiology and neurology that made Einstein such a towering intellect. Whenever they discovered something they thought was really cool, they would call me over to the table to investigate alongside them. I can clearly remember my first introduction to the microscope. I was looking at a piece of Einstein's brain and I was utterly amazed by how clearly you could see its cell structure (even though, at age 8, I had no idea what a cell was or how it functioned).

The biggest lesson I learned from Mr. Harvey's work comes from the fact that, even though he was an extremely accomplished pathologist, he worked in uncharted territory. Einstein possessed genius greater than any other man he had ever examined, so Mr. Harvey couldn't necessarily rely on his specialized knowledge to detect what was so remarkable about one of the greatest brains that ever lived. Because he didn't know what answers he was seeking, he had to concentrate his efforts on asking questions, which is something even I was capable of doing at such a young age. Moreover, Mr. Harvey couldn't possibly have made any discoveries without the aid of my father, whose work as a physicist afforded him a way to develop the unique instruments Mr. Harvey used. One of the most important things to learn about innovation is that innovators don't work alone. I learned this at an early age by watching the brilliant teamwork between two scientists as they worked at uncovering the genius of another.

❧ ❧

I had yet another teacher of innovation, Dr. Melvin Gottlieb, who was the director of the Plasma Physics Laboratory in Princeton, and who lived just down the street. He was the head of the university's efforts in trying to perfect nuclear fusion as an inexhaustible supply of energy. Some of the devices he and his team built were the size of train cars, and they used staggering amounts of electricity to smash atoms and make them fuse together. As were all of my mentors, Dr. Gottlieb was great with handling children, which made him an expert at explaining why it took such big machines to manipulate things as little as atoms. It puzzled me terribly to imagine that atoms were too small to be seen, so Dr. Gottlieb took time to teach me about the relative sizes of things in the universe: how things can be as small as atoms or as large as galaxies, and still coexist.

≼ ≽

I had many mentors who taught me that we can indeed see things we never thought we could. Dr. Hans Winterkorn, my neighbor and a professor of civil engineering at Princeton, was also the leader of my Cub Scout den. All our meetings were held at his laboratory on campus because he knew that little boys are truly fascinated with scientific things such as learning how to make buildings out of sand and concrete. He predicated, quite correctly, that we would be even more captivated by learning how things such as hurricanes and tornadoes tear down buildings.

One Saturday morning, he built for us a small replica of a building sitting on a bed of sand. It looked stable enough, but then he added a modest amount of water to the sand. Without a word, he caused a small oscillator to start vibrating, and, within seconds, the building toppled over (much to our delight). Dr. Winterkorn demonstrated to the den that soil can literally liquefy in the presence of water in fantastically few seconds. It would have taken him hours to explain the mystery of this phenomenon on a blackboard. But he was wise enough to know that what you hold in your hand, you never forget.

Learning how to innovate means tearing down the barriers in your mind that say there are achievements automatically off limits in a specific time or space. Even something as grand-scale as a skyscraper-toppling storm can happen in the middle of a simple Cub Scout den.

❧ ❧

I learned similar lessons from my next-door neighbor, Professor William Feller. He was one of the world's leading experts on probability and statistics at the time, and today, his books are classics as well as textbooks for modern-day thinkers; their examples are extremely lucid and relevant. Yet, as I kid, I only knew him as the nice man next door who adored gardening. I used to love to go over and look at the beautiful plants he had growing all over his property; I especially loved his magnificent daffodils. Dr. Feller would ask me questions such as, "If I plant 10 daffodils, what do you think the chances are that they will be the same color when they bloom?" The following spring, he would show me what had sprouted. By moving probability into a world that I could touch and feel, he made it come alive.

I still use these examples when talking to my 10-year-old son and his friends, because early childhood is the best time to learn about a universe of things too tiny or too humongous to see. Believe it or not, children are much more open to acknowledging what they cannot see in their own range of vision. After all, children are constantly changing size themselves. Being able to think in such flexible terms is a crucial component of innovation, because this allows the mind to search for solutions in places that otherwise might seem too out there or too insignificant to consider.

These same men also taught me that even things we can't see can still be proven real. Right down the street from my house lived Professor Seymour Bogdanoff, professor of aeronautical engineering at Princeton. He had a really fabulous wind tunnel out at the University's Forrestal Labs. On extremely special occasions, he would take me out to the site to watch the experiments leading up to supersonic and hypersonic flight.

I was seriously into model airplanes at the time, so those trips were a dream for me. Dr. Bogdanoff taught me that even things I couldn't see—air, for example—can still have massive and wonderful implications on the way things (such as airplanes) work. During one of these trips he explained to me that no one could have ever innovated the airplane if he or she worked only with materials he or she could see. Until I started listening to him, I truly believed that, if you could not see something, it did not exist. Learning to let go of this, I learned one more piece of innovation's puzzle.

❧ ❧

One of the biggest things that cripple the would-be innovator is fear. Most underdogs feel justified that they have a lot to be fearful about. Underdogs are usually fearful that they won't make enough money to support themselves and their families, that their educations or job titles won't let them be innovative, or that attempting to think up a million-dollar idea would prove to be a failure. These are all fears of the adult world, but, in my book, they have no relevance at all in the world of innovation. Children can teach us a lot about how to keep fear from conquering the innovative spirit (and this is not because they are fearless). Young people acknowledge and process fear much differently than adults do; ironically, a child's perspective on fear is much more productive than an adult's.

In retrospect, a situation from my own youth serves as an excellent example of how to regard fear and doubt as an adult. When I was in high school, I was absolutely addicted to 45 rpm records, but being able to purchase the amount I was convinced I needed became next to impossible to accomplish on my allowance alone. So I started to look for a part-time job in my community, and, eventually, I found work with Professor Harold Gulliksen, a mathematical psychologist at Princeton. He needed someone to keypunch data for input into his computer. In the old days, this was accomplished with a very complex and intricate 80-column punch card. The task was tedious, and Dr. Gulliksen kept me busy for weeks on end, just entering data in the very same precise and ordered form. The job kept me happy; it could be monotonous and tiresome, but it was a routinely predictable way to pay for my 45s.

But one day, Dr. Gulliksen called me to his office and pointed me towards a sheaf of papers covered with a bunch of odd-looking words and strange symbols I could not comprehend. He handed me a thin little manual and said to me, simply, "This is a programming language called Fortran. I want you to learn it and then create a program to process these equations I have for you here. I've got to go away for a week so please have it done by the time I return."

I was absolutely terrified. Over the previous weeks, I had come to see Dr. Gulliksen as my mentor. I was in awe of the complexity of his work and the elegance with which he carried out his experiments. Inputting his data, I'd become thrilled by the prospect of someday having my own laboratory just like his, where I could conduct my own experiments and hire some young man like myself to arrange the critical data I discovered. Now, the man that was my inspiration was going away, and he was leaving a task in front of me that I was certain I was incapable of doing.

45

But, for all my worries, I got the project done just in time for Dr. Gulliksen's much-dreaded return. In hindsight, when I thought about how I managed to accomplish the task in just the right amount of time, I realized that I got it done because I was prompted by the only type of fear that has the capacity to motivate.

I was certainly scared when Dr. Gulliksen packed up and left that day, leaving me with a mountain of foreign work. But I was never scared of the work itself. Like any young person hoping to live up to the expectations of his or her guide, I was really only terrified of not being able to do what was expected of me in the appropriate amount of time. I was never scared that I couldn't make the symbols make sense; I was panicked that I wouldn't be the ideal apprentice for one of my heroes.

Here is the crucial lesson about fear I learned from that experience: The only way to deal with fear is the way a child would. An innovative person focuses their fear on what will happen if the task is not accomplished, not the task itself. If you do this, the stories in your life will have a happy ending like the stories in mine: One day when I was in college, I ran into professor Gulliksen after not having seen him for years. He invited me back to his office for coffee, and when we got there he took out a copy of his latest book. He autographed it for me with the words, *this is the result of analyzing the data you wrote the programs to do.*

❧ ❧

A lot of adults mistakenly believe that being innovative means taking control of the universe and making it do precisely what you would like it to do. But this is absolutely not the case. An innovator is not as much in the driver's seat as most people think. Rather, an innovator is a passenger riding in a car through the processes of nature. The things that give the innovator his power are his ability to pay attention to where his journey through the universe can take him, and his knack for drawing connections between different parts of the world.

Another one of my high school jobs involved washing glassware in the laboratory of Dr. Jacques Fresco, a professor of biochemistry at Princeton. Dr. Fresco eventually revealed to me that he didn't just hire anyone to wash his dishes; he said he had detected an aptitude for chemistry in me for a long time, and so it wasn't long before he invited me to become a technician in his group. He was studying the nature of RNA and how it was involved in the transmission of genetic information in cells. The source of the RNA he studied was regular old bakers' yeast.

The biggest part of my job with Dr. Fresco's group was helping him score the subject of his experiments in the middle of the night at a warehouse just outside of New York City. The operation sounds suspicious, but it was actually as innocent as a bunch of post-doctorate fellows picking up yeast alongside all of the New York City bakers who needed the stuff at midnight to start baking for the day. Though making the yeast deal was quite guiltless, this didn't mean we didn't attract the cops like crazy on the way home; all the yeast bubbling over in the backseat made the entire car smell as if it had been washed in beer.

When we got back to the laboratory, Dr. Fresco would lead the team all night in treating the yeast with a sequence of chemicals to extract the RNA before the cells died. I learned a lot from this process about the very essence of life as it appears in the genetic material of the very simplest organisms. I even found the opportunity to

47

use this information in a project I entered into the Westinghouse Science Talent Search, the nationwide science fair in which I came in sixth place. As a finalist, I got to meet President Lyndon Johnson, who joked to us that he was especially happy to meet us because his daughter Lucy had told him that morning, "Brains are in this year, Daddy."

Even though I received a mountain of scientific experiences from my work with Professor Fresco, the most important thing he ever said to me was that "Mother Nature will reveal her innermost secrets if you ask her nicely." Treating nature with the respect that it deserves, such as appreciating the wonder that exists even in the simple cells of organisms such as yeast, is something we learn as children and something we should cling to if we ever hope to be innovative adults.

❧ ❧

The greatest thing about my childhood, the thing that should be the greatest part about anyone's childhood, is that it never stopped being a part of my entire life. By this I don't mean that I simply remember the events of my childhood and cherish all my past experiences. Rather, I believe that part of what has made me an innovator is that the fact that I carry my childhood around; I keep my inner child, my underdog, with me at all times.

Children often find themselves in trouble because they are extremely unassuming. Though they have rules and regulations placed on them all the time, children naturally see no limits. If you can remember the story of "The Emperor's New Clothes," you'll recall that the emperor marched through the streets of town completely nude while the crowd of adults remained too embarrassed and scared to point out the absurdity. The strip show didn't end until a child screamed out that the king was as naked as a jaybird. The fable doesn't specify whether this child was punished royally or not, but children who speak so frankly in the real world aren't usually let off the hook. Yet, looking past social codes, rigid rules, and ultra-strict criteria is something children do and should never stop doing if they are to become successful adults.

When I was not so much a child anymore, I went off to Harvard University for graduate school. My third day there, I heard about a group conducting research work on blending computer science and organic chemistry. The group was exactly what I wanted to focus my own studies on, so I determined to be a part of it. The leader of the group was Professor Elias J. Corey, one of the world's leaders in his field (he won the Nobel Prize in chemistry in 1990), and, if I hadn't been raised to ask so many questions and seek so many opportunities, I would have been right scared of the man's genius.

Instead, I thought it would be a good idea to show up at his office one day and tell him I was all ready to be a part of his group. Professor Corey was a bit taken aback when I shared my decision with him; he stared at me for quite a bit before he finally said quietly, "The way it is normally done, is that you would submit a transcript, go through and interview, and then ask my permission to join my group."

I was pretty frightened that I had overstepped my boundaries so much that I'd get the boot from Harvard my first week there, but then Professor Corey leaned back in his chair, smiling, and said, "Well, as long as you are here and you have an interest in the project, welcome to the group." Professor Corey lived up to his reputation of brilliance as long as I worked with him, and he taught me many invaluable techniques to fostering innovation, some of which you will read about later in this book. Most importantly, though, Professor Corey influenced my future career as an innovator by encouraging me to pursue my dreams filled with gusto and free of intimidation.

Most people are never really "well-rounded," but the time of life when most people come closest to this ideal is childhood. Most kids are encouraged to play lots of sports, join many clubs, study a variety of subjects, and clean their plates of an array of different foods, all in order to create minds and bodies capable of tackling life from many different angles. As kids, we were taught not to put all of our eggs in one basket, yet it seems that as soon as we graduated high school we were told to pick a major, pick a job, and stick with the program until the monotony made us old. This way of life is the death of our inner innovators.

❧ ❧

After I finished graduate school, I accepted a job offer from the DuPont Institute in 1974. It was there that I met Howard E. Simmons, an extremely accomplished chemist who was director of the Central Research Department. Indeed, he was a man of such extreme breadth and intellectual scope that he was not just an expert chemist; he had published literature on his other areas of expertise from mathematics and topology to Mayan cultures and the reading and writing of their hieroglyphs. The most important thing I ever learned from Dr. Simmons, however, had nothing specific to do with math or the Mayans. Instead, the most invaluable thing he ever said to me was, "You have to be an extremely focused scientist if you want to keep your job at DuPont, but, if that is all you are, leave now. I expect—no, I demand—that the researchers at this institute have as great a passion for other things as they do for science."

So many people believe that truly innovative scientists accomplish so much by locking themselves up in their laboratories all day long to pore over their materials. But restricting yourself to one realm of life or science will not ensure you enough knowledge to create wonderful innovations; in fact, it will guarantee you'll do the opposite. Innovation involves drawing from every stretch of the planet, bringing technology or processes from one part of life to change the nature of another. I certainly don't limit my range of thinking to the realm of computers; in fact, anyone who knows me is privy to the fact that I spend as much time with my bichon frises as I do with my research. We can learn how to be innovative from all walks of life, even those which haven't been grown in a laboratory. Creativity and innovation are inspired every day by the most unlikely creatures; I know because my pups, my underdogs, were the inspiration for this book.

You might be thinking to yourself, "Well of course this guy turned out to be an innovator; he grew up around people like Einstein!" There is a lot of truth to this statement, but not the kind of truth you might think. Yes, I learned a lot from the brilliant men I was surrounded by in my youth, but the things I absorbed were not necessarily the complex concepts of their science; I really benefited from the essence of their spirits. From my mentors, I learned to be grateful, to be respectful, to be fearless and bold, and to dive passionately at least once into all the oceans of life. These are lessons anyone can learn. Think of yourself as caught up; you have now learned as much from Einstein as I have, and you are ready to innovate a better world.

Chapter 4

Innovation Meets the Westminster Dog Show: Selecting the Right Innovative Breed

Believe it or not, opening one's mind up to innovation is similar to experiencing the joy of attending the Westminster Dog Show. Innovation is a multi-fractioned field: there are so many types of innovators, so many kinds of innovations, that the variety compares to the hundreds of breeds that show off their stuff at New York City's prime canine event each year. And just as you don't have to be a company big-leaguer to innovate, you don't have to be a perfectly coiffed terrier to win "Best in Show" either.

In 2008, a cheerful little beagle named Uno became the first of his kind to win the coveted Westminster Championship. A century of "Best in Show" competitions had never before produced a winning beagle; until recently, judges didn't award dogs of this breed for their loud vivacious personalities, their endearing attachment to their owners, and their very sincere commitment to being man's best friend. Uno sure didn't have the typical qualities of a winning show dog; his simple chestnut mane was no match for the poodle's expertly shaped 'do, and his relatively small stature lacked the command of the massive mastiff's frame. Yet little Uno couldn't be ignored. He maximized the beagle breed's charm by baying and whooping his way to a win; with this he changed the Westminster Championships forever.

As an innovator, you will surely differ from other creative thinkers in the strengths and weaknesses you bring to the table. Some innovators are rich in education and teeming with knowledge so specialized it can change the way the technological world works. Others might have brilliant business mindsets capable of maximizing production; even more might excel in recognizing patterns of sameness and putting information together in new and completely unique ways. Still others might have such strong senses of culture and people that they are able to predict where the world will be in the future, and what man will ask for next. The point is that, no matter what kind of life experience and education you have, there is a field of innovation that's yours for the taking. And your chances of success are the same, whether you're a little beagle or a giant Great Dane.

The following is intended to outline just some of the ways the underdog can approach innovation using his or her own unique talents. This list of innovation "breeds" is by no means exhaustive, because innovation is an incredibly plastic science; creativity can be harvested from more places than we can ever expect. Just as a dog can be born from infinite combinations of breeds, innovations can be composed from many different approaches to creative thought. Take a look through this compilation as you would go shopping for a dog: appreciate each variety of innovation for its own attributes, think about which suits your style best, and, if you don't find exactly what you are looking for, remember that you can always breed your own innovative method.

⊰ ⊱

When most people think of innovations, they generally picture the "product" variety. This is reasonable; most innovations are performed on products. A product innovation is generally defined as a change to a product (or service marketed as a product—think iTunes) that makes that product different, more efficient, or less expensive. An excellent example of a truly beneficial product innovation is that of controlled release pharmaceuticals, drugs that only need to be taken once a day instead of every few hours. Even though they are considered to be lifelines by most, drugs are still indeed products. As with most merchandise, they must be constantly improved upon and marketed more efficiently in order to make their manufacturers an ever-increasing amount of money. Drugs undergo product innovations all the time; even once-a-day prescriptions are being surpassed in the world of birth control, where women can now implant, insert, inject, and even adhere their medicine to their bodies.

Product innovation advertisements are all over the place; you can usually spot them by recognizing some key words common to most product-innovation marketing campaigns. You've almost definitely heard of product innovations that are "longer lasting" (deodorants), "more effective" (laundry detergents), or "less expensive to operate" (hybrid car engines). A lot of these upscale products are true to their claims: worth their weights and your while. New chemical combinations really do make it possible to smell fresher longer while getting your clothes and keeping the environment impeccably clean. But not all product innovations live up to the notion of "new and improved." This happens for a couple of easily recognizable reasons.

First, it is very possible to *over*-innovate a product; more is not always merrier. Think of a symphony orchestra and the delicate blend of carefully selected sounds that go into producing a truly beautiful piece of music. What would happen if the orchestra was to add new instruments to its ensemble for no other reason than it was asked to? Just because a few members of the audience might like to listen to guitar doesn't mean the conductor should usher in a rock star to "complement" all of the other string instruments; such a sound would be terrible. Similarly, adding too much to a product in order to exploit each and every quality it could possibly possess can often lead to a big mess. Sometimes all of the new innovative features of a product don't get along.

There is a lot of logic behind the conventional wisdom that says one should never purchase a new car model the first year it is manufactured. I've twice had this experience, and, believe me, it's not fun to be a car company's guinea pig while it sorts through all of a new model's bugs. It's important to remember that not all of a product's potential features will work in harmony; in order to have an efficient product you have to prioritize. If you are developing a new kind of car, you have to choose whether your priorities lie in creating extreme fuel efficiency or manufacturing mega horsepower. If you try to do both, your efforts might end up broken down on the side of the road.

Likewise, improvements to innovations, especially those related to precious human biology, don't often come without side effects. When you hear one of those colorful commercials enthusiastically promoting a new drug for acid indigestion, at the risk of sudden seizure or death, you're best to believe the advisory is serious (if only somewhat sincere). The prescription drug market is constantly being bombarded with new miracle cures for minor ailments that are either no more effective or much more dangerous than old medications. Of course, more new drugs are *supposed* to mean more money, but this kind of logic is exactly what you want to avoid when you are innovating a product. Profits should never singularly inspire products; profit motivation is a no-go for both producers and consumers because, ultimately, a bad product will always lead to financial loss for everyone. (Think about all the lawsuits that "new" drug will incite after hundreds of patients have seizures over upset stomachs.)

Believe it or not, people who are product-minded innovators are such because they are good at one simple and fundamental human behavior: complaining. This is because the very first step in innovating more efficient merchandise involves determining what's wrong with what already exists. Cultivating a critical eye for sub-par products should come easily once you've realized that the world and its goods aren't perfect. And anyone who's purchased anything, from a new car to a new toaster, knows that most products don't work the way they are supposed to. Some people deal with these scenarios. They learn to eat burnt toast, and they surrender themselves to submitting their cars for repairs once a month. But other people, purebred product innovators, are put off by poorly produced products. These folks take it upon themselves to find better ways to make almost anything. Product innovators have healthy egos; they've got enough confidence to speak up when a product stinks, but they are also open-minded enough to search any- and everywhere for solutions.

❧ ❧

You don't have to be a product innovator to sell your ideas. Process innovations, amendments that enhance the way things are done, are just as easily packaged and marketed as products. For instance, Microsoft's new operating system, Vista, can be purchased, boxed and shrink-wrapped, off the shelf. However, though it is sold as a product, Vista really functions as a novel process, a new system for managing computer information.

Vista exemplifies another way process innovations are similar to product innovations: They are both easy to mess up. To call Vista an ineffective process innovation would be an extremely polite understatement. It is important to remember that, just because a process innovation works, doesn't mean it *works*. Vista's capabilities are fully functional, yet they are so invasive and awkward to navigate that people tend to turn off the program in order to spare themselves the aggravation it causes. When an innovation is too annoying to operate, it might as well not work at all.

The world has seen many great process innovations—ones that have lived up to their creators' intentions by making the world faster and more efficient. For instance, though the nutritional integrity of its menu is debatable at best, most people will agree that the fast-food system found at McDonald's is the best way to get a customized, satisfying meal in relatively short time. Because this system is so effective, it keeps being improved upon. For instance, a startup company in Pittsburgh, Pennsylvania, has found a way that technology can make fast-food lines even faster: it has developed a system that can take your order before you even open your mouth to place it. The business proposed a way to innovate the standard drive-through television system so that it might assess each car's passenger content for advanced order preparation. Simply put, if the system detects an SUV and determines multiple heads are inside, it presumes that the occupants are children and instructs the staff to start assembling Happy Meals ahead of time. Conversely, if the system sees only a single head in a high-powered sports car, it calls for the staff to start making a more macho meal. Published reports say this system will increase drive-through service time by a double-digit percentage. If McDonald's were to implement the system in all its restaurants nationwide, the chain would surely rake in a huge profit. Just think about how many times you've abandoned the idea of a Big Mac because the car line was wrapped around the building. With the new television system, McDonald's might make customer profiling a big way to bring in more business.

Not all process innovations are as effective as the new McDonald's drive-through operating system. For instance, a lot of people appreciate the self-service gasoline pumps that allow a user to insert a charge card and process the transaction oneself. The procedure creates what could be a win-win situation for both pump owners and their customers: The former saves money on lower labor costs, and the latter saves a whole lot of time (conventional wisdom tells us time is money). Though many people might be content with the new status quo, I can't help but remember how gas was serviced in the good old days. Way back when, a stop at the gas station meant drivers not only got to fill their tanks, but they also got to have their windshields washed and even their oil levels checked. When I remember how gas stations used to be, I can't help but think that the industry is now too focused on fixing something that was never actually broken in the first place. Sometimes I wonder how many fewer accidents the world would see if everyone's windshields were just a little bit cleaner and their engines were routinely serviced. Maybe time *isn't* money when time saved means safety sacrificed.

In general, good process innovators have a great deal of (justifiable) impatience. They cannot tolerate doing things one way when another method is quicker or easier. Oftentimes, contrary to what you might think, process innovations aren't driven by the leaders of big corporations; the need for a process innovation is usually first detected by workers at the bottom of a company, those who are caught in the thick of things. In the case of the McDonald's innovation, it might be that the monotony of hamburger assembly could actually be the perfect catalyst for creative thought. No one is better suited to innovate new ways to serve customers than the restaurant worker whose job is to interact with impatient, hungry hamburger-eaters all day long.

❧ ❧

Yet another type of innovation is the service innovation. Generally, service innovations deal with changes in information, interactivity, or ease of use. It can get a little tricky at times to differentiate service innovations from process innovations, but a good way to distinguish one from the other is to remember that process innovations are designed to bring in more sales by decreasing the time it takes to make them, whereas service innovations bring in more sales by keeping customers from going crazy.

An excellent example of an efficient service innovation is the Medco Company's system for ordering prescription refills. Before drug companies began utilizing the Internet, refilling prescriptions was an absolute nightmare of red tape and convoluted phone calls. Now, companies such as Medco have taken nearly all the hassle out of a formerly painful process. With its innovative Internet refill service, a few clicks of a patient's mouse (24 hours a day and seven days a week) can provide the company with enough information to put the order through.

Because service innovations are geared primarily at making purchasers feel valued and at ease, the effects of a bad service innovation are perhaps the worst for a company and its customers to deal with. Consider the automated telephone service selection tree, the "press one for such and such," "press two for so and so," and so on and so forth without any number one can press to talk to a human being. "Please listen closely, as our options have changed" is a phrase that sends most patients, clients, and customers through the roof. It seems that, no matter how a service's options have changed, they never correspond to the assortment of reasons a person would call up a business, store, or office in the first place. The arrangement is a wolf in sheep's clothing; selection trees get callers nowhere while pretending to cater to their every need. The end result feels extremely patronizing.

People who are great service innovators are usually great process innovators who have a little something special. They are sensitive folks who know what makes customers feel good and what makes them insane. Good service innovators realize that customer satisfaction depends on a lot more than just product or process efficiency; taking care of customers can contribute just as much to whether or not they feel good about their purchases.

❖ ❖

Yet another type of innovation deals with organizations. Organizational innovations are geared at changing how an entire entity is structured and/or how it interfaces with the external world. Big companies are far more than just the sum of their parts; they are almost like living, breathing organisms, entirely dependant on and influenced by even their tiniest components. Ironically, many qualities of large modern-day companies and organizations are quite similar to those of prehistoric dinosaurs. For example, a fully grown dinosaur reached physical proportions that were massive relative to its tiny size at birth. As an enormous adult, a dinosaur's nervous system would get so sluggish that the reptile might hardly feel anything during an injury, perhaps only a slight tickle in a leg a Tyrannosaurus had tried to rip off. Likewise, as a company grows larger, it feels less pain when something goes wrong. It is much easier to ignore an inefficient employee if he is one of a thousand than if he is one of 10. Organizational innovations are such that they help companies work better as a whole, even as they grow to greater and greater proportions.

An exemplary organizational innovation can be seen in a remarkable company called Gore Associates, the developer of GoreTex, that famous clothing material that sheds water while preventing the feel of a steam bath at the same time. Gore Associates had already innovated a way to keep the physical bulk of clothing from suffocating its wearers. Its fabric innovation was showing fantastic efficiency, but soon the company grew to such a size that employees were losing touch with each other and innovating less. In order to keep its proficiency, the heads at Gore Associates decided that their employees needed to be better acquainted with each other. So that their employees might keep producing their best work, the entire company subdivided itself into "sites" that were restricted to no more than 300 employees each. When a single site grew beyond its allotted number of workers, a whole new site was constructed, and a subset of the old site's personnel was moved to occupy it.

From firsthand experience, I know that it is a real joy to recognize, and be recognized by, the head of the entire site where you work. Numerous surveys have shown that, because of the way it organizationally innovated itself, Gore is a highly ranked company in terms of employee morale and efficiency.

You might think that all companies would benefit by copying the Gore organizational model to achieve the same high-efficiency levels. But organizational innovations are just as unique to different companies as product innovations are unique to the different gadgets they improve. A company that produces athletic apparel will need to be structured quite differently than one that manufactures gourmet ice cream flavors; the types of positions needed and the amount of employees working together in groups are factors that are completely different in every business, even those within similar markets.

❧ ❧

Too many businesses have neglected to innovate their own unique organizational models; in effect, they've all failed miserably by trying to copy other companies' systems. Here's a great example. I used to work for a prominent chemical company that was in major need of its own organizational innovation. The flaw in its system was that it utilized isolated groups of sales representatives for each of its different product lines. Because each product model was represented separately, customers would sometimes have to consult with five or six different sales associates before they felt confident enough to make a purchase. This entire arduous sales process created a landfill's worth of unnecessary paperwork for the company; at the same time, it deprived customers of the opportunity to leverage different purchases for better discounts. In order to save its sales, the chemical company restructured itself so that each of its sales associates was trained to represent every product line. The change resulted in much lower costs of sales, better use of customers' time, and more efficient scale and scheduling.

Though the reorganized sales strategy was exactly what this particular company needed, the technique was certainly not designed to be "one size fits all." However, soon after the chemical company made the change, a big computer company tried to structure itself the same way. The results were disastrous. Because of the nature of its products, the computer company understandably had less synergy between its software, hardware, and services lines. This fact made economies of scale harder to achieve. In addition, it was a huge challenge for the computer company to find sale representatives who understood its radically different product offerings. The company had to revert back to its old organizational structure quickly, but not before it acquired some level of damage. It takes a very long time to build up customer confidence; it takes very little time to lose it with a bad organizational innovation. Running a successful company requires much more than the innovations behind your products and services. It is also very much about how wisely you innovate your entire organization. Good organizational innovators are people who can keep track of an entire company's living parts, ensuring that they work together most efficiently.

❧ ❧

When you set up shop to sell your innovation, you've got to be ready to do business. When most people consider the word *business*, they usually envision either a dull, dry set of motions or a morally corrupt system of connivance. But the heart of business is actually very dynamic and creative. Doing good business isn't about choking your customers to death for all they're worth. It isn't simply about setting and collecting a price for your product either. As a living, breathing organism, your company should keep shedding its skin and growing larger and more efficient; businesses are just as subject to "survival of the fittest" as people are. Therefore, as the head of your company, or even as a member of someone else's, you should constantly come up with new ways to innovate the way your organization does business.

A business innovation is any change in the way a product is offered that helps it capture more value. This effect can be achieved by a slew of methods: decreasing your costs, making your organization more attractive to customers, or even performing a service for other companies. Remember that, even if two companies adopt the same business policy (such as a two-for-one offer to increase overall sales), one business's innovation will always be unique from another business's innovation; each must be tailored to fit the specific company.

Telephone companies are particularly genius at creating and expanding great business models. To see this, all you have to do is consider your cell phone. If you are similar to most people, you probably paid for a basic, pay-by-the minute plan the first time you signed up for cellular service. As cell phones became more popular, service companies offered more sophisticated plans that allowed customers to pay for an allowance of minutes per month; this way (in theory), customers could more carefully budget the minutes they consumed. With this modification to their original business models, phone companies also granted themselves the license to penalize customers for going over their allotted monthly minutes. The whole arrangement benefited customers who actually paid attention to their plans and followed the rules; those people received package discounts on minutes while using a predetermined amount to curb their spending. The business model certainly worked for the phone companies. Customers usually signed up for more minutes than they planned to use in order to give themselves buffer minutes between those they actually planned to consume and those that would end up costing them 99 cents per pop.

Not too long after traditional talk plans became the status quo, text messaging became the mode of communication even more beloved than the traditional phone call. Because of this shift, phone companies felt the pressure to innovate their business offerings so that customers could chat online, text, or talk on the phone with the same device. They began offering customers instant-messaging services along with a certain amount of messages, free of charge. Any additional messages could be purchased, just as cell phone minutes could, in package deals. Because customers were already familiar with this model, they began to gobble up instant-messaging plans as quickly as phone minutes.

The evolution of cell phone service is very much alive; mobile devices are constantly being updated with the latest and most convenient service technologies possible. People can now use their phones to surf the Web, check their e-mail, download ring tones, and customize wallpaper. Each different company offers slightly different deals on these phone "extras"; customers can purchase two services for the cost of one, more service for exponentially less money, or a new service feature with an extended trial period. Though a cell phone company might make money when you purchase that new camera phone (a product innovation), it will make a much greater profit on your new two-year contract with unlimited text messaging, Web browsing, and instant messaging (all business innovations). This situation demonstrates the importance of business innovations; sometimes they will bring in more profits than any change you could make to the actual product you are selling.

∞ ∞

Because business model innovations are so important, it's crucial that your company or organization goes about undertaking them the right way. As can all other types of innovations, business innovations can go very wrong—to the point from which it's hard to recover. For instance, for a long time, all government roads were owned and operated by the states through which they ran. The state governments paid to have their roads constructed, and they maintained them by charging drivers tolls to cover operational costs. Yet in recent years, several states have fundamentally changed this model by selling their roads to private companies. The thought behind this change is that the road sales provide quick cash that governments can use to cover current obligations, and/or eliminate the need to raise taxes.

On the surface, selling roads for these reasons might seem to be a good idea, but the change might actually turn out to be a very disastrous plan of action. Once its roads have been sold, a state government no longer has the power to make sure the roads are maintained properly; the private company then has the power to determine how much maintenance will keep the roads in good operating condition. If the company does not fulfill its obligation, the state government has very little recourse; the legal process to compel the company to compliance is arduous, at best. There is also the danger that the company could go bankrupt after letting the roads deteriorate far past the point at which they are safe to drive on. At this point, the government could always take the roads back, but it would cost a tremendous sum to complete the backlog of repairs necessary to restore the roads to their proper function. Additionally, if the company had such problems running the roads, the government could have just as much difficulty keeping them up (especially if it was compelled to sell them in the first place). This is a scary scenario, and hopefully drivers in all states will never have to experience it. However, this hypothetical and all-too-possible crisis situation serves to show the almost irreversible damage a bad business model innovation can create. Good business innovators are sensitive to the idea that evolution works forward, not backward; once a business has changed its model, it is nearly impossible to turn back.

❖ ❖

Somewhere between developing an innovative product or process and growing a large and successful business around your creation, you will have to think of some innovative ways to meet marketing success. Marketing innovations are those that help a company attract more customers to the product or service it is trying to sell. An excellent example of a fantastic marketing innovation is the customer rating system implemented by online shopping sites such as Amazon.com. Whether you want to buy a book or a lawn mower, Amazon makes it easy to research the quality and reliability of the product you're looking to purchase. A five-star rating system, plus a catalog of customer comments (ordered by chronology, helpfulness, or satisfaction), make it a cinch to comparison shop between different products based on what real people have to say about them. This marketing innovation is certainly a huge contributor to Amazon's incredible business, because, essentially, the Website has invited customers to act as salespeople for other customers. There is (so far) no better, more honest way to attract more buyers than this.

Most times, the simplest way to innovate a company's marketing campaign is to offer a discount, or, better yet, something for free. If you've ever known someone who just cannot resist a sale, then you know how successful discounts and freebies can be. However, it's not impossible to poorly integrate discount prices into your marketing innovation plan. For instance, a local bank near my home once offered what, on the surface, seemed to be a very worthwhile promotion to attract more credit-card customers. In order to encourage more card signups, the bank instituted a program that converted dollars spent to points redeemable for merchandise or gift certificates. However, the bank foiled its own marketing ploy by instituting a "cap," a maximum number of points that could not be surpassed no matter how many dollars a high-spending customer charged.

In theory, the bank must have believed it was doing itself a favor by limiting the rewards it might have to pay out. But, in reality, the bank's policy became an incentive for its customers to avoid the cap by spreading their business among other organizations. If the bank had thoroughly thought out its marketing innovation, it would have realized that the point system wasn't worth the hassle unless customers could exploit it to its full potential. Essentially, the gimmick punished the bank's best customers. A good marketing innovator is one who knows how to create situations that benefit all customers proportionately.

❧ ☙

Once your company has established its unique business model and innovative marketing campaign, it must be able to creatively and efficiently distribute its product to its customers. In short, your business must be able to create its own supply chain innovations. As can now be expected, Amazon.com is one of the clearest examples of an excellent supply chain innovator. Back during the days of old-time retail chain stores, Sears Roebuck made a fortune selling its own branded merchandise in both its stores and its catalogs. But today, a company with such a homogenous inventory won't find a fraction of the success enjoyed by a business that retails merchandise from all over the world. Amazon.com completely revolutionized the supply chain status quo by transforming itself into a one-stop shop. Instead of wasting hours of time using Google to find the best vendors for particular items, a consumer can simply let Amazon act as his or her storefront to an entire world of goods. Just type in "treadmill," and Amazon won't just provide you with hundreds of models' worth of "burn" for your buck; it'll buy and ship from each vendor, too. In a sense, the site supplies its customers as a personal shopper would; just search, and it seeks out in less than a second—with delivery overnight.

Unfortunately, I once worked for a chemical company that really damaged itself and its customers by needlessly "innovating" a new way to supply its merchandise. The following is a classic illustration of the very useful saying: "If it's not broken, don't fix it." It is also very clear proof that technology can (ironically) often make existing processes much more complicated.

At one point, this company decided it would save itself time and money by allowing its customers (mostly scientists) to place their orders using a Web-based system instead of over the phone. The company thought this supply chain innovation would save its customers from callbacks and telephone tag while simultaneously eliminating the cost of its sales clerks' salaries. It was theorized that the PhDs placing orders were certainly intelligent enough to fill out their own product requests;

there seemed to be no need to pay high school–educated clerks to complete the task for them.

However, eliminating the clerks from the company's team eventually produced a classic catastrophe: Not long after the new self-service ordering system was in place, a biochemist decided he needed to order 500 rubber bulbs. However, when he went to place his order, he did not realize that he had to divide his desired quantity of bulbs by increments as small as a dozen or as large as a thousand. Because of this oversight, he requested 500 *cases* of 1,000-count rubber bulbs by mistake. Because there were no clerks to manually oversee this process, the order went through without a hiccup, and the supplier surely swallowed hard when he saw the massive order for 500,000 rubber bulbs. The bulb manufacturers went into "red alert" in order to meet the requested shipping date; they had never needed to produce such a quantity so quickly. However, the panic they must have experienced measured nothing next to the surprise felt by the scientists; they were utterly shocked when three 18-wheeled trucks pulled up in front of the research building to drop off rolling hills of rubber. When all the numbers were added up, this one mistake cost the customer almost 10 times what the company thought it would save by eliminating its clerks. Surely, this scenario shows how a poorly thought-out supply chain innovation can go terribly wrong. It also illustrates how a good supply chain innovator appreciates all employees' roles in successfully distributing products to customers.

❖ ❖

One last innovation sub-type is perhaps the most interesting of all. Social innovations are those that improve peoples' lives by changing how they interact with one another. Today, we can see many examples of social innovations around us, such as PayPal, speed dating, and even Facebook. But perhaps the Oscar of all social innovations goes to the biggest Internet phenomenon of all: YouTube. Ten years ago, most people would have laughed at the thought of a billion-dollar home-video Website; yet YouTube has become just this. The brilliance of this site rests in its creators' expert assessment of society's needs and desires. YouTube caters to young parents who want to share home videos of their children with Grandma and Grandpa living thousands of miles away. It also allows talented youngsters to show off their singing, dancing, and acting talents to potential fans, agents, and scouts all around the world. YouTube makes it possible for users to share thousands upon thousands of funny, educational, or just plain fascinating videos on one big, easy-to-operate Website. YouTube realizes a universal and previously unfulfilled need for video communication. It seems everyone (except, perhaps, some hermit high up in the Himalayas) knows of and thoroughly enjoys YouTube. As a 1.5-billion-dollar investment, it's worth every penny: YouTube has become the heart of the Internet, pumping users to sponsor sites all over the World Wide Web.

Social innovations seem simple enough; the thought process behind YouTube is obvious in hindsight. Most "why didn't I think of that?" ideas are social innovations, yet this innovation breed is much trickier to master than it looks. Society is built upon the ebb and flow of cultural trends and whether or not a social innovation meets success can depend heavily on the seemingly smallest things. In a way, social innovations are very similar to fashions: There are many styles of jeans in the world, but often, one particular shape—the bellbottom, the boot cut, the skinny leg—is usually the go-to trend of the season. All jeans serve the same basic clothing functions (protection and modesty), yet the subtlest difference in contour about the waist, pockets, or legs seems to make all the difference when it comes to which fit flies off retail shelves the fastest. This same principal applies to social Internet innovations. We live in an age in which it seems no one can get enough of Web-based networking sites such as MySpace and Facebook. What, then, happened to the first of all social networking sites, Friendster?

There are many theories that attempt to explain why Friendster flopped in the face of other social networking sites. Some people blame the Website's not-so-catchy name. Others say Friendster failed itself when it declined Google's 30-million-dollar offer to buy it out. Though the second scenario certainly seems more damning than the first, it still doesn't explain why Friendster was incapable of rising to lasting success on its own.

In order to figure out why Friendster fell from grace while MySpace and Facebook skyrocketed to popularity, it's best to compare social networking sites to society as one would compare different jeans to a body. When it comes down to it, Friendster really failed because its features were just not tailored well enough to fit its users' demands. Friendster's biggest priority was showing how members knew each other through social trees connecting friends and family. However, social networkers were never as concerned with analyzing precisely how they knew friends as they were with just meeting as many people as possible. Because Friendster's site was preoccupied with constantly calculating social relationships within four degrees of separation, its load time became significantly slowed. Eventually, as Friendster accrued its first one million members, it began taking more than a minute of its users' time just to jump from one profile to another. And it turned out that networkers were much more interested in looking at profiles based on their users' interests and/or attractiveness—not just by social networks. While MySpace especially offered this type of consensual Internet voyeurism at rapid speed, Friendster struggled to keep its social connections clear in the face of ever slowing load times.

The Friendster scenario shows us that new ideas aren't exempt from the constant process of tweaking and fitting to best meet customer demands; if you don't shape your own design, sooner or later someone new will come along and make the adjustments for you. Just because Levi's made the first jeans doesn't mean it sells the greatest amount. Just because Friendster became the first online networking site doesn't mean it has the most members. Good social innovators know that ideas must be developed to find the best fit. And a lot of times, this process depends on society's "seasons."

❖ ❖

You should now be familiar with all innovation breeds. Most importantly, you should be able to recognize the beauty and significance of each type of innovation, from those that improve products, to those capable of changing society. Depending on your talents, you might be purebred for one specific type of innovation over others. You might even find yourself a bit of a mutt—capable of undertaking many types of innovation at the same time. Regardless of which breed of innovation you choose to pursue, remember that they are all important enough to win Best in Show.

Chapter 5

Fetching the Right Facts: Discovering the Appropriate Innovation Information

One of the most frequent and fervent questions I'm asked about innovation is this: What kind of education is required of an innovator? The general consensus is that a person has to learn a whole lot about a ton of different fields before he or she will ever be able to improve any of them. Wherever I speak, most people expect me to leave them a laundry list of educational essentials they'll need in order to discover innovation (in the very-far-off future). But the fact of the matter is that education can hinder innovation as much as (if not more than) it helps it along. And what can be so detrimental to innovation is not just the misuse of formal education, but also the mishandling of knowledge gained from everyday experience. Letting yourself get carried away with all of the solutions to a problem can prevent you from getting at the heart of the problem itself. In this chapter, I will show you how efficiency is most crucial to successfully recognizing and solving a problem, whether the issue you're tackling exists in the realm of computer technology or the parameters of your personal kitchen.

❧ ❦

When discussing how the right amount of education contributes to effective innovation, it is first helpful to distinguish between two major types of innovations: those that deal with procedures and those that are based in technology. Unfortunately, most people think that there is only one kind of innovation: the technological type. It is true that this form of innovation can only be accomplished by highly skilled and technologically savvy folks. For instance, the scientists who figured out the autopilot function on a jet plane had to manipulate knowledge and machinery existing completely outside of the realm of normal know-how. Yet although the puzzle pieces with which they had to work were extremely complex, the way in which they assembled the entire puzzle was actually quiet simple and standard. These scientists didn't have to innovate autopilot as a new process of motorized movement; they merely had to take the concept of autopilot from other modes of transportation and integrate it within the specialized technology of jet planes.

However, innovations often abound outside the realm of any specific science. Procedural innovations are those that can be accomplished by any member of society, regardless of his or her occupation or education. And these innovations are no less important than their high-tech counterparts. In fact, procedural innovations are often credited with making a lot more money.

For example, one of the greatest, most recent innovations is the creation of one-click ordering on one of the world's most popular Websites, Amazon.com. Essentially, what Amazon created was a way for a consumer to store credit card information on the company's online database so that each successive purchase he or she made could be paid for at the click of a button. Coming up with the concept of one-click ordering required absolutely no specific knowledge of computer or Internet technology. It did, however, require an extremely fine-tuned appreciation for the psychology of the online shopper and the anatomy of an impulse buy. What the innovator of one-click ordering knew, the rest of us should all (unfortunately) know, too: People spend a lot more money when they don't have to think too long and too hard about it. By reorganizing online ordering to better exploit the consumer's desire for "painless" purchasing, Amazon was able to rake in millions more for an idea anyone could have come up with.

Another example of a non-technological, procedural innovation is the microcap bank. Institutions such as the Grameen Bank in Bangladesh are microfinance organizations that provide small group loans to impoverished people with ample skills but no collateral. Although the innovator of the microcap bank, Muhammad Yunus, is an economics PhD and a Fulbright scholar, his innovation didn't require any type of specialized knowledge other than a belief in the underutilized abilities of the poor and an overexposure to the horrors of poverty and famine. Because of its founder's philosophy, microcap banks are popping up all around the globe and generating hundreds of billions of dollars from almost perfectly repaid loans. Because its services have rescued so many people from drowning in poverty, the Grameen Bank won the Nobel Peace Prize in 2006.

Often, even innovations that are based heavily in technology are just as deeply dependant on procedure.

If people aren't able to come up with new ways to implement their knowledge, they'll find that their expertise will eventually become stale. For instance, innovating a drug to cure a new type of virus requires the most advanced knowledge of the application of chemistry. But just as a virus might mutate and reorganize itself in a new and uniquely devastating way, so must the drug that overtakes it come from a novel application of medicine. The trouble is that most scientists don't think as the enemy does: Diseases are programmed to constantly innovate new ways to kill people, whereas scientists can get stuck in the rut of trying to treat all diseases by implementing the same methods they've researched and found success with. Having extensive knowledge of a specific kind of science can make one so secure in that capability that it becomes too easy to ignore outside ways of thinking.

❧ ❧

It's common for people to think that successful people stick to what works. To a point, this is true, but the secret to everlasting innovative success is being able to stretch your mind outside of your comfort zone for new solutions. Even though what you're doing might be working for you at the moment, there is always a high chance that you'll discover a new and different way of doing things that will work even better. And it is almost a guarantee that what works now won't work forever; this is why looking for prospective solutions ahead of time is a must. (Think about how crucial it is for today's generation to innovate new ways to use energy so that tomorrow's generation will have a place and the provisions needed to live.) This is why an improperly handled education can actually stifle innovation: The more you know, the less likely you are to come up with a breakthrough innovation that uses your knowledge in a unique and important way.

However, the less you know, the less able you'll be to innovate based on facts and reason, and the less successful you will be than even the highly educated fellow who is stuck in an innovative rut. The discrepancy between too much knowledge and not enough seems to be the classic catch-22 situation, but in reality the two extremes serve to delineate a specific playing field on which innovators can seek out and employ just the right type and quantity of knowledge.

The first step in mapping out the mind for innovation is probably the hardest. It requires that the innovator stay grounded in the problem he or she is attempting to solve before jumping ahead to look for solutions. An innovator must be able to clearly define the problem's boundaries, what exactly needs to be solved. Believe it or not, one can actually over-solve a problem.

Think for a minute about the awful complexity of contemporary computer software. Most pieces of programming consist of multiple dimensions of features layered on top of one another. Some of these features are absolutely requisite to a program and useful to all of its users. However, other features are specific, and useful to a limited group of users. For example, many components of popular word-processing software programs come into being when groups of professionals request that software be encoded for a particular task that is useful to their particular work. The problem with this situation is that the more extraneous features there are in a program, the more hoops the average user has to jump through in order to use its fundamental functions (hence the more time needed to get a relatively simple job done).

Thus, trying to make your innovation super-efficient can actually leave it barely functional. For example, currently there are several thousand commands in Microsoft Word, though informal studies have suggested that typical users employ less than two dozen to get their work done. Even so, Microsoft continues to test as many combinations and permutations of commands as they can, to relatively little avail and a great amount of problems; it seems every new release of the program has been riddled with a ton of bugs.

I have some degree of sympathy for what Microsoft is trying to do; I encountered the same problem of over-complicated software while revising Raptor Systems' Internet firewall. Fine-tuning an innovative product is in many ways similar to finishing a great piece of art-work: You have to know when to stop. Just as a formerly breathtaking canvas can be spoiled by a superfluous brush stroke, a usually high-performing piece of software can be ruined with too many pieces of code.

❧ ❧

When my company first began marketing the Raptor firewall, we were pretty eager just to see our product sell. This means that, whenever a paying customer asked us for a new feature, we added it, quickly, because we knew we needed revenue to pay the bills. In order to protect our sales, we let our customers dictate how many features we added to our program, without considering whether or not each of the additions would weaken the function, integrity, and security of our system. Because we jumped the gun to add almost anything and everything our costumers could conceive of, we eventually ended up with a great mess.

Raptor Systems became what is gently referred to as "spaghetti" software: programming composed of components so tightly intertwined that singling out any individual function is almost impossible. After a while, Raptor became so overwhelmed with extraneous code that it was on the verge of collapse; the support costs it took to run the extra features completely overwhelmed the marginal increase in sales the additions brought in. Eventually we had no choice but to spend a painful amount of time completely rewriting the whole code, this time paying attention to logical, efficient design instead of listening only to impatient costumers. By the time we finished reducing Raptor Systems to its most productive package of features, we were astonished to find we'd reduced it to half its size (while increasing its speed by a factor of three).

The lesson we learned here is the supreme value of being able to define which problems to solve and which not to. When developing any innovation, the underdog must realize that he can't fetch an answer to every man's problems. Attempting to do so is a definite pathway to bankruptcy because it means spending a great deal of time and money to produce as little as one additional sale. And this isn't worth it to either the producer or the consumer.

❖ ❧

Innovation does not rest on specialized knowledge alone; nearly all successful innovations are built upon the innovator's ability to selectively use (and not use) the information available. Many innovations don't require any specialized information at all—there is a whole world of undiscovered procedural innovations just waiting to be realized by everyday underdogs who may not even have formal educations. Innovation is about practicality and prioritization, knowing when to build on top of your idea and when to focus on what you've created already. As with everything else, good innovation is about moderation.

Where else is moderation a bigger issue than in the kitchen? Believe it or not, a great exercise in smart innovation is yours to learn by throwing a simple dinner party. Consider this scenario: You are going to host an evening get-together and you've invited a bunch of friends for a home-cooked meal. Do you decide to prepare individual dishes to suit everyone's taste, or do you plan a menu from which the guests can choose? You might think that preparing individual dishes would be the best way to please each and every one of your guests, but in reality you'd being doing everyone a favor by planning a menu with several selections and letting each guest find his or her best match. This is because unlimited dishes require unlimited trips to the grocery store, unlimited pots and pans, unlimited cooking times and temperatures, and thus very limited patience for each and every nitpicky visitor. In reality, the fewer ingredients you use, the more creative you will be, and the more likely it is everyone at your party will enjoy his or her food.

When it comes to throwing a top-notch dinner party, your success might rely less on your cooking skills than you think. Just as a scientist with a great amount of knowledge can overlook the simplest ways to use it, a great cook with the most ingredients in the kitchen can get so bogged down with each complicated combination of flavors that he or she can't get all the dishes to the table at the same time. Too much information, like too many ingredients, can really mess up innovative creativity.

Likewise, too little information can send a person in all the wrong directions while he or she tries to find solutions (in a petri dish or a pantry). It's obvious how ignorance can be unproductive to the scientist, but it is just as detrimental to the would-be host or hostess. Have

//

you ever gone grocery shopping for an event without even thinking about a specific menu? This is just as dangerous as going to the grocery store when you are stark-raving ravenous; you'll want to buy everything in sight. Thus, upon returning home to your kitchen counter, you will have acquired a ton of ingredients (material knowledge) and very little insight as how to put them all together.

This misstep in menu planning represents one of the greatest mistakes preventing innovation in all fields: trying to solve the problem before you've even defined it. Heaving a ton of miscellaneous ingredients onto the chopping block to make a dish is like pulling out everything you know in any order to solve a problem—completely ineffective if you haven't clearly defined what the situation requires. You don't necessarily need a lot of exotic ingredients to make a great dish or a lot of fancy knowledge to create an elegant solution. When you are throwing a dinner party, your objective isn't to create an award-winning combination of flavors. Rather, your mission should be to entertain a specific group of people with a specific grocery list in a specific amount of time.

Once you really, truly know what your problem is, you should start writing down all of the characteristics a solution to your dinner problem should have. You may well find that this step takes you in an entirely different direction than you would have originally thought. It could be that your solution requires a whole new cooking paradigm. A lot of time it's not the ingredients (knowledge) you have, but how you put them together (procedure). Perhaps stir-frying one or more courses instead of broiling or baking them is the only way to get the job done. This could very likely be the case if you realize you cannot cook two things in the oven at the same time (especially at different temperatures). You might also come to select your menu based on common inter-mediate steps between different courses (perhaps a sauce and a dessert both require eggs, one needing yolk and the other one whites).

Only when you have all this mapped out should you then go to the grocery store; at this point you will know exactly which ingredients to buy and in what quanti-ties. And if you just have to buy that novelty ingredient, looking so tempting stacked beautifully atop a mid-store food sculpture display, at least you will be able to asses the impact it will have on the rest of your meal.

If you want a fun and tasty way to learn how to apply the right knowledge to innovation, try integrating the right ingredients into a dinner party menu. Host an event that requires each course to use the exact same set of ingredients (though perhaps in different ratios). Because this is an experiment, I suggest you only invite some of your closest friends. Insist that each guest (or couple) be prepared to cook one course in your kitchen, all at the same time. It is great fun to watch as the "play-ers" of your party try to figure out how to cooperate and share resources while everyone is driven by the same primal urge: hunger. Whether you permit wine or beer as a pre-dinner innovative lubricant is up to you.

◅ ▻

Where does this leave us? In order to innovate, you need a certain amount of detailed learning—somewhere between a pinch of wisdom and a cup of knowledge. You need to have the right kind of kitchen (sandbox, labora-tory, workshop, and so forth) to bring your concept to prac-tice. Most of all, you need the courage and self-confidence to truly believe that your ideas are worth pursuing. Sure, you will encounter lots of times when you discover your idea has already been brought to market. But this does not diminish the value of your thought processes, and it doesn't mean you're stuck. Real innovators know how to work with what they've got; there are a million ways to cook with the same ingredients.

Chapter 6

Manipulating Materials: How the Underdog Innovates With Both Simple and High-Tech Resources

Often I find myself bumping into old prototypes in or on the desks, shelves, and closets of my home. Many of the designs are discovered half completed and collecting dust from decades before. Though I never purposefully abandon any of my innovations (unless of course they are terrible ideas), my life is so filled with creative prospects that, more often than not, I am forced to temporarily sacrifice one innovation for the development of another. Most new innovators would scoff at such a scenario; the under-confident underdog often feels so stiff and empty in his attempt to generate just one new, novel idea that the notion of feeling full of original concepts and short only of time to pursue them all might seem absurd.

Rest assured (even if still in minor disbelief) that once you have been fully captured by the life of the creative thinker, you too will have more ideas than you'll know what to do with. Learning innovation is not just about overcoming the initial obstacle of getting your brain in the right mode to create. Even after you've done that, you will be forever challenged to prioritize all of your ideas by how successful—commercially, lucratively, or personally—they will be at any given time; you should then be able to pursue them in that order. As your confidence and productivity increase with your ever growing arsenal of original innovations, you will have to become an expert at determining which ideas to put all of your stock into at the present moment—and which to put down to delve into later. These decisions can be hard to make. Thankfully, your life's circumstances should make these choices relatively painless.

❧ ❦

If you want to learn how to prioritize your innovative pursuits, just look to the principles involved in the simplest game of cards. If you, for example, are playing a particularly lucky game of rummy and find yourself with three-of-a-kind sets of 8s, 9s, and Queens, you might be tempted to put all your cards down in one impressive play just because you have them. But, in some versions of the game, you may only put down one set of cards per turn. Though this may seem to be just an arbitrary rule, this policy actually makes room for higher total scores. If you play your Queens for the maximum points first, there is always a chance that the cards you draw in subsequent turns will allow you to play your 9 of hearts with the face cards of the same suit later on in the game. In the end, you will have scored more points for yourself than you would have with your three-of-a-kind 9s.

You should follow this same rule in the realm of innovation. When it comes to organizing how you will tackle all of your ideas (and trust me, this time will come), it is best to play first the prospect that promises the most in the present. You will always be able to keep your other cards (ideas) tucked away in your hand (messy innovation closet) and play them at a later date. This way you will be able to give all of your innovations the time and attention they deserve while reaping the maximum rewards for yourself. If you explore your larger, more immediately promising ideas first, some of your seemingly smaller ideas could shock you later with all of the wonderful and varied uses passing time and thinking brains might discover for them.

Recently, while I was doing a bit of spring cleaning, I came across an innovation I'd completely forgotten about. When I tried to recall the details surrounding the advent of the idea, I remembered that I was working on the design at just about the same time I began developing my firewall. (This explains why this perfectly good idea had to find a seat on my brain's backburner for the time being; Internet firewall security was just too hot.) Shortly before the advent of Raptor Systems, I'd been toying around with an idea aimed at assisting my wife in the war she'd been waging with her jewelry wardrobe. Her particular problem was the way the back of her earrings dug into the side of her head whenever she talked on the telephone. It didn't matter what style of earrings she wore; whether they were simple, diamond studs or long chandelier sparklers, the back of her earrings were all the same: sharp, pointy, and very prone to stabbing the soft spot behind her ear when pressed by the hard, plastic earpiece of any telephone.

It seemed that the only available solution to the ear pain problem was for women, including my wife, to take their earrings out before participating in phone conversations. However, the arrival of an important phone call is very rarely predictable, and removing a pair of earrings isn't always possible before picking up the receiver (especially when a person is talking on a cell phone on the go). To boot, doing this often results in losing the earrings. Oftentimes the effort to prevent earrings from digging into the side of one's head results in stepping on a lost pair later on and feeling them stab into one's foot. Many people have learned to live with this uncomfortable scenario; for decades, women all around the world have grown used to either chronically losing dozens of earrings or slowly drilling tiny circles into their skulls. But I only needed to step on one pair of fishhook earrings, long lost in the carpet on my living room floor, before I knew I had to make a change. Having one's foot impaled by 2 inches of thin, sharp, vicious metal is quite enough inspiration to innovate.

After extracting my motivation from the sole of my foot, it seemed almost immediately obvious to me that such a simple problem required only a rudimentary solution. Though the earrings that had been troubling my wife were certainly not inexpensive, that didn't mean that the means to prevent them from hurting her or going AWOL in the living room carpet had to be costly as well. And even though each jewelry accessory she owned was unique and one of a kind, that too didn't mean that my earring innovation had to be assembled with hard-to-find, specialized materials. Though my firewall innovation dealt with cutting-edge, fresh technology, my earring innovation solves a problem so ancient that its construction can be accomplished with a simple trip to the hardware store. In order to extinguish earring agony for women all around the globe, all I needed was a little foam, adhesive, and felt—materials that have been around since the Stone Age.

After some simple experiments with size and shape, I was able to develop the Ear Saver. The final design consisted of a donut of soft foam with a layer of felt on one side and a layer of adhesive on the other. It was constructed to be attached by its sticky side to the earpiece of any phone, so that when a person's ear touches it, the soft layers of felt and foam conform to the shape of the earring; the "give" inherent in the cushion is so that the earring can relax into a customized pocket on the receiver instead of cramming against the ear and forcing the back of the earring into the head. Producing the devices was a walk in the park, as they cost almost nothing to make; all I needed to assemble them were a couple quick trips to craft/home appliance stores. I made dozens upon dozens of them in a matter of days, and, soon after, my wife and all her friends ate the donuts up; fastening them to their home telephones and cell phones was a cinch. I was pleasantly surprised when my testers told me that the device packs in even more bang for its (very minimal) buck: It also functions as a noise shield, which makes background noises less noticeable: Thus the Ear Saver makes talking on the phone a lot less painful in a variety of ways.

I was just about to commercialize the idea when Raptor Systems took off and I had to prioritize my innovations. And it's a good thing I did. If I hadn't tackled the firewall right then and there, I would have missed out on the perfect time and place to bring the world my cutting-edge idea. Internet security was a fresh, new issue, but lethal earrings have been around almost, it seems, since the dawn of time. If you are choosing between pursuing an innovation that has been missing for decades and an innovation that is needed in the immediate present, go for the latter. Ironically, chances are good you will be able to go back to the innovation that should have been generated way before your time. (As you will see in Chapter 13, the longer a problem has existed, the less likely people

are to believe that it can be solved. Therefore, when innovating a solution to an "older" problem, your competition
is greatly reduced.)

I am glad I let the Ear Saver sit around for a bit; my
11-year-old son is now at the age at which he is eager to
enterprise. The gem of this innovation is that it has
multiple markets; it's possible that he will be able to
sell the Ear Savers to jewelry stores and phone companies alike. But the most important thing to understand
about the Ear Saver is that it is essentially just a new
use for an old material. Fundamentally, the Ear Saver
is a cushion. People have been using cushions for centuries to add decoration and comfort to their furniture. In
the last century or so, cushioning material has been innovated to suit other areas of life such as packaging and
shipping. With the advent of airmail, cushions have come
to be made of materials other than leather and lace; now
cushions can consist of almost anything from paper to
foam to inflatable plastic (bubble wrap). In developing
the Ear Saver, all I had to do was let my brain realize
that the solution to the problem at hand was probably
already out there; I just had to tailor it to suit my particular need. Sure enough, I only needed to realize that
the earring issue presented just one more of the many
undiscovered applications of cushioning material.

❈ ❈

You should always expect to find multiple uses for
just about every material you encounter. Believing that
one type of matter has only one use will put a huge
damper on your innovative spirit. The belief that materials are exclusive to only one application is absolutely
incorrect, whether you are in a laboratory or even in
nature. Consider the world of the truffle. Truffles are
exotic, especially flavorful mushrooms that grow in the

underground area around the trunks of oak trees. Because the delicate truffles flourish beneath layers and layers of earth, the only way to detect them is through the incredibly sensitive noses of pregnant pigs. In order to collect the coveted truffles, a farmer must take his pigs out on leashes into a forest. As soon as the pigs begin digging around the base of a tree, the farmer pulls them off, provides a distracting treat, and then digs up the truffles.

What makes truffles special are their incredible flavor and aroma. What makes them *incredible* is the vast and varied number of dishes they can contribute to. Truffles can be served raw and sprinkled over hot pasta dishes and gourmet salads. They can also flavor meats as stuffings or marinades, accent foie gras presentations, and enhance spreads, cheeses, and pâtés. The truffle's flavor has been synthetically replicated in truffle oil, and its notes have even been used in top designer perfumes. It is exactly this breadth that makes truffles a challenge to chefs everywhere. There are a lot of enthusiastic diners to be won by the restaurant whose chef comes up with the next unique truffle creation. The same is true for the innovator: The next great idea is likely to be a dish that makes an old ingredient new again. Think of innovation as a chef would think about incorporating truffles into his next culinary creation. A huge part of innovation requires you to discover how an old material can flavor a new area of life.

Truffles abound in the world of technology just as well as they grow beneath trees. An example of a particularly fascinating technological truffle I've worked with is the expandable miscrosphere. This little high-tech treasure has so many uses; its known applications may even outnumber the delectable dishes that can be created from truffles. And, silly enough, I discovered the miscrosphere as a result of shopping with my wife for shoes.

One day, a while back, I was sitting down to a pretty typical meeting with my boss at DuPont when he remarked that I looked a bit more stressed than usual. Quite suddenly, and without much hesitation, I was compelled to recount for him the horrible shoe-shopping extravaganza I had endured the day before. I lamented how much time I'd spent waiting in the women's shoe department of six different stores, watching my wife select a few styles, try them all on, walk about the store in each pair, and finally put every shoe back on the shelf because none fit "quite right." I told him how my wife and I had returned home later that day, after driving many wasted miles and significantly elevating our blood pressures, with no new shoes to speak of. I had vowed right then and there that I would find a material that could be incorporated into the lining of shoes so that the shoes themselves could be adjusted—either thermally or otherwise—in-store so that every customer could find his or her perfect fit in one trip. I needed to develop a material that was lightweight and expandable— what is now referred to as a "microsphere"—and I needed help to do it.

My boss felt sorry for me (he, no doubt, had experienced the same thing with his wife), but he had little interest in pushing my idea to the top of the company. (Indeed, he had many other opportunities stacked above my microsphere prospect.) I, however, was very serious about not having to go through another shoe shopping crisis ever again, and so I took it upon myself to consult with all the appropriate powers elsewhere in DuPont about my idea. I was disappointed (but hardly dissuaded) when I was eventually informed that DuPont had no interest in becoming a shoe materials manufacturer. The effort to develop the kind of technology I was after would not have proved lucrative enough for DuPont; the profit from such a product would have gone almost entirely to the shoe designers and retail stores. Though DuPont's rejection of my proposal was a small bump in the road to realizing my shoe innovation, the decision was right for the company. It also served to illustrate an important lesson about innovation: In order to get your innovation produced, you must be able to make the idea worthwhile for the manufacturer and/or developer. The way to do this is to come up with as many uses for your innovation as possible. If, for instance, DuPont was not interested in developing microsphere technology for use in shoes, I could have presented another application of microspheres that would have made DuPont's work with the technology worthwhile. The point here is that the more uses your innovation has, the greater the likelihood you will be able to attract both buyers and manufacturers.

Fortunately enough for everyone involved, I discovered that a variant of microsphere technology was commercially available from another company. Once I retired, I was able to purchase my own quantity to experiment with to my heart's content (while taking care not to violate any of DuPont's confidentiality policies by using any of their trade secrets). Here is the heart of what I believe is one of the most wonderfully useful discoveries of modern technology: The active ingredient in microspheres is the conglomeration of thousands of small, hollow, plastic spheres filled with an inert liquid under pressure. When the spheres are heated, they soften, and their pressurized liquid contents cause them to expand to roughly three or four times their original diameter—about 50 times their original volume.

When the heat source is removed, the plastic outer coating hardens again, yet the microspheres are able to maintain their new, larger size. Because they are spherically symmetrical, they cannot collapse, even after they've grown. Try uniformly compressing a ping-pong ball; you cannot do this for the same reason a miscrosphere cannot cave in after it's been enlarged through heat.

Because I was so excited about the potential abounding in microspheres, I determined not to do the technology a disservice by pursuing only a couple of its applications. I decided to challenge myself to see how many ways I could revolutionize the way the world worked using only my little plastic spheres. The first step in this process was the most important: I had to make sure I completely understood the physical properties of the microspheres before I was able to imagine their potential uses. Getting carried away with how I wanted to use them before I even knew what kind of material I was attempting to manipulate would have severely hampered my innovative efforts. So, after I analyzed them carefully through observation and data, I was able to devise a list of clear, concise qualities that made microspheres something special.

Boiled down, they are particles that are roughly the size of face-powder components. Microspheres are extremely stable, both chemically and physically, and they can be expanded enormously with the application of only a modest amount of heat. Finally, they are extremely lightweight, and, when expanded, exhibit amazing resiliency. This information means that microspheres offer us the opportunity to make existing products lighter, expandable, better able to withstand shock, and capable of releasing stored chemicals.

After I was thoroughly versed in what microspheres are made of, I was ready to assemble my list of their potential uses. The list of applications that I eventually conjured up is far too expansive for me to conquer completely on my own, so the information that follows is completely free for your creativity to handle. Make a note here that many different people can come up with multiple innovative uses for the same material; do not get intimidated by the work people have already accomplished with any specific substance. The chances are that, if the material has already been manipulated a hundred ways, it can just as easily be manipulated a hundred more. When you are innovating with an already-existing material, be sure not to concentrate on how it is currently used as much as you concentrate on its nature—this objective strategy will allow you to exploit your subject in the most new and original ways. Also, as you will see, you do not necessarily need a high-tech team or a cutting-edge laboratory to find new uses for an existing material. Sometimes, you can innovate simply by sitting down at the dinner table.

❧ ❧

I happened upon my first original innovative application for microsphere technology quite unexpectedly. A friend of mine invited me over for dinner one night, and, as we sat down to enjoy the delicious meal she had prepared, she asked me what I initially thought to be a ludicrous question. She first explained that she had recently watched a documentary about the success of gastric bypass surgery in helping the morbidly obese lose weight. She said that, although the surgery did seem to improve the lives of many people, she couldn't help finding fault with the severity of the procedure, its association with some pretty horrific side effects, and its astronomically high cost. She also pointed out that, ironically, the more overweight a person is, the less likely he or she will even be a good candidate for the surgery.

Gastric bypass surgery requires anesthesia, which can be downright deadly if given to a patient whose heart is already overstressed. (An overweight person's heart is almost guaranteed to have suffered chronic strain because every unnecessary pound makes a person's heart work that much harder.) After presenting all this information (and causing me to eat my meal much more cautiously), my friend asked me to consider how my material, a powder with the consistency of talcum, could actually replace weight-loss surgery. Had she been a professional colleague, I probably would have dismissed her with a litany of technical objections; I honestly did not think I could answer her question. But because she was a friend who had made me a nice dinner (even if her topic of conversation diminished my enjoyment of it), I decided to be more open-minded toward her prospect.

Though I was initially skeptical of her idea, it was soon clear that her question had unwitting depth to it. As I began to mull over how I could make her request a reality, I started to consider other circumstances in which people swallowed inedible materials. I started to think about drugs. I began to ponder how illegal substances are smuggled into the United States. One of the most common ways this is accomplished is for the drug to be poured into latex condoms, which are then given to a "carrier"—often called a mule—to swallow whole. While the mule travels across the border, the condom travels through their digestive system, and, when the mule has reached the dealers' destination, the condom is retrieved from their feces and the drug is extracted and sold.

I began to imagine how this process could be combined with microsphere technology in order to create the same feeling of satiety that ensues from gastric bypass surgery. Eventually, I discovered how microspheres could work in place of invasive weight-loss procedures: a slightly porous, condom-like container, about the size of a large vitamin tablet, could be filled with microspheres and swallowed. Once consumed, the microspheres would expand at the temperature found in the stomach. If an obese patient were to swallow one or more of these pills, the pills would lodge themselves in the stomach, where they would become too big to exit into the small intestines. In this position, the pills would help generate a feeling of fullness even after the patient ate only a small quantity of food. After the patient lost the desired amount of weight, a surgeon could laparoscopically slice open the container so that the microspheres would be released into the intestines and harmlessly passed through the body. The microsphere procedure would involve minimal scarring, no permanent side effects, and none of the risks associated with serious surgery; hence the treatment would possess none of the downfalls of gastric bypass surgery, while harvesting all of the results.

❧ ❦

I discovered a second opportunity for microsphere technology in a similarly unexpected way. A few years ago, after months of painful procrastination, I came to terms with the fact that I needed to remodel one of my bathrooms. Because I am a hands-on kind of guy, I decided that I was more than capable of laying a new tile floor myself. However, after a few failed starts, I was disappointed to discover that the DIY projects that seem a cinch on the shows of HGTV and the DIY network require special skills very much outside the realm of a simple PhD. As I embarked on the project independently, I noticed very quickly that my tiling talents were not up to par. Though I have bad astigmatism, I could clearly see how terribly crookedly I was positioning the squares as I worked across the floor. Eventually, I purchased many of the plastic X-shaped corner templates to help keep my tiles straight, but I was soon frustrated with how much more tiresome they made my work; every tiny tile required four X shapes lined up back to back, and the tedious time the device added to the application of every single square made it hardly worth the effort. (If I'd kept up with the Xs, my back would have collapsed before I finished half of the floor.)

I also had serious issues when it came to grouting the tiles: Applying a thin but tenaciously sticky layer of cement between very small segments of ceramic is absolutely not my area of expertise. Unfortunately, grout sticks to a floor tile's shiny surface too easily, and the excess takes ferocious work to get off. If the tiles are colored, as mine were, the slightest unevenness in the layer of grout is extraordinarily obvious. Finally, once the floor settles underneath the tiles, after they've been applied by an amateur such as me, it's a guarantee that the grout will crack, quite visibly, while losing its water tightness.

After botching up my bathroom floor more times than I care to tell, desperation took hold of me and I decided to mix my microspheres with some flexible silicone caulk. Once the two were combined, I used a rolling pin to flatten the concoction out to the thickness of my floor tiles; I then cut the mass into narrow strips, as if I were making pasta. With these few simple steps, I was able to revolutionize my whole tile-laying process: All I needed to do with my new "grout" mixture was alternate a strip of caulk with a row of tile, and so on. The caulk strips were cut to be straight and of consistent width; because of this, I was able to lay the tile rows perfectly straight within the boundaries created by the perpendicular and parallel caulk pieces. When all of the tiles were down and the cement beneath them was dry, I only had to run a hot hair drier over the lines of caulk to finish the job. Because the caulk was mixed with the microspheres (fully expandable when heated), the hairdryer caused the caulk to expand both horizontally and vertically so that it formed a watertight, uniformly high seal against the pieces of tile. As an added bonus, the flexibility of the caulk meant zero cracks as the floor beneath the tile settled.

As I considered how the expandable microspheres helped me tile my floor without any cracks, I started to think about other ways in which the microspheres could make other landscaping and/or building materials more durable. All I had to do to discover my first idea was sit on my back steps to ponder the issue. Before I even had the chance to establish a clear line of thought, I was perturbed by the fact that my back steps were riddled with cavern-ous cracks. I knew that this was because the steps were constructed out of concrete. In the winter, the precipita-tion that penetrates concrete will freeze and expand as the temperature drops low enough to turn water to ice. This water expansion causes large cracks in the concrete that can be unattractive and downright dangerous. Many years ago, the construction industry discovered that leav-ing a small number of air bubbles in finished concrete greatly increases its durability by providing room for expansion and contraction. However, these air bubbles naturally attract more water, which greatly weathers the concrete to the point where it must be replaced for top dollar. The U.S. government has estimated that the replacement of weathered concrete—of potholes, cracks in buildings/sidewalks, supports for bridges, and so on—is costing the economy tens to hundreds of billions of dollars a year.

If microspheres were to be used in concrete mixtures, they might totally revolutionize the construction industry by eradicating the problems of concrete weathering and disintegration; microspheres allow room for expansion while keeping water out—that's exactly what they did for me. To upgrade my back steps, all I needed to do was mix several large handfuls of microspheres with concrete powder. The spheres did exactly what I had hoped they would do, and my improved set of stairs is still incredibly sturdy and sans cracks years later. As an added bonus, the microspheres made the concrete lighter, so working with the material left me much less fatigued than I would have been with the old-fashioned stuff. It is worth it to note that my stair refurbishing was a small-scale project, and therefore relatively inexpensive. A larger-scale project—perhaps the construction of a whole office building—might require tens of thousands of dollars spent on the microspheres alone. Although cost might be an issue, this doesn't mean that microspheres won't pay off in the long run. Building a structure that lasts longer and uses less energy (the spheres are little insulators too) is always more morally *and* fiscally responsible.

❧ ❧

These are just a few of the ways I was able to directly enhance my own life by innovating with a multitasking material. Because microspheres can be purchased off of the shelf, other creators have had the liberty to do some fantastic things with them. Here are a few of the most innovative and influential uses of microspheres for your own innovative inspiration:

☞ Microspheres are used in anti-slip coatings to increase friction and prevent accidents.

☞ Microspheres are used in Braille paper to produce three-dimensional patterns.

☞ Microspheres are used in auto body fillers and putties to reduce weight while improving sandability and application.

☞ Microspheres are used as a bulking material in electrical cables in order to improve electrical insulation.

☞ Microspheres are used in civil explosives to increase sensitivity and uniformity.

☞ Microspheres are used in cultured marble to reduce weight, making marble furniture and fixtures easier to transport and/or install.

☞ Microspheres can be incorporated into the soles and heels of shoes to make them lighter by more than a pound—a true improvement when this 1 pound is multiplied over thousands of steps a day.

There are potentially a thousand more uses for microspheres out there; those discoveries are all for your taking. Though it might seem that an innovator must discover a completely new material from which to construct an original innovation, some of the most brilliant designs have been fashioned from stuff that's already out there—from high-tech microspheres to commonplace foam and felt. You are the artist, but you don't have to create colors in order to paint a brilliant piece of art.

Chapter 7

The Answer Is Right Under Your Nose: How the Underdog Taps Into His Natural Instincts

Curiosity may have killed the cat, but it is the life of the underdog. After you've defined a problem, your obvious next step is to find an innovative solution. But finding the creative spark to light a groundbreaking fire doesn't require you to crack open your skull and pick apart your brain for traces of genius. In fact, you needn't look for solutions inside yourself at all, because the answers to all your questions abound in the world around you. Simple curiosity about the processes and nature of our world is what inspires the genius inside of every underdog. Innovation is not a miraculous byproduct of some extraordinary cognitive process. Rather, innovation demands only that the innovator consider his or her surroundings and put its raw materials to use in a novel way.

The two most essential ingredients for innovating are: first, familiarity with the things in daily life that cause you frustration, and second, curiosity. These two elements inspire all discoveries and innovations. Though most people associate curiosity with the relatively carefree lives of children, pure, effective curiosity can actually be a difficult skill to master. Being curious means being open to the possibility that things are often not what they seem to be. Curiosity is critical to innovators in each and every field, even those that seem grounded in solid science. Frequently, curiosity requires us to seek solutions outside of our comfort zones, in areas unrelated to our realms of expertise. Even innovators at the top of the medical field need to broaden their horizons in order to find solutions to the most specific and complex problems.

❧ ❧

An example of the curiosity factor at work in the world of medicine is the innovative new treatment for stomach ulcers. A stomach ulcer is a sore in the sensitive lining of the digestive tract that occurs when the integrity of the stomach's protective coating is compromised and acid is allowed to antagonize the tissue underneath. For as long as most people can remember, the occurrence of stomach ulcers was blamed primarily on stress and the consumption of spicy foods. The assumption that emotional distress causes stomach ulcers was based on a very real, naturally and commonly occurring phenomenon.

We have all likely felt our stomachs "burn" after hearing terrible news or while anticipating something awful to come. Physiologically, it seems to make sense that stress could disrupt our stomachs enough to cause ulcers. When the human body is under extreme duress, the brain cuts off blood flow to less-essential organs such as the stomach in order to preserve energy for use elsewhere. Because stomach mucus production depends on blood flow, it makes sense that stress would compromise the stomach's level of protection and allow acid to eat away at its tender lining. However, though stress might make ulcers feel worse, ulcers are just as present on an island vacation as they are behind the work desk. Even if cutting stress out really did cure painful ulcers, it would still be a less-than-desirable remedy. Stress is a natural part of life; it even abounds in the most fundamental tasks of raising a family and holding down a job. Therefore, cutting back on work and family time is a solution that would probably cause more ulcers than it cures.

In the past, ulcer victims were still miserable even after they modified their meals. In vain, ulcer-prone people almost grew used to subsisting on diets of cream soups, macaroni and cheese, and pizza without the tomato sauce. The theory behind using a low-acidity diet to treat ulcers was also grounded in logic: Acidic foods might combine with stomach acid to further erode the stomach's protective coating, giving way to ulcers. However, dietary sacrifices often offered little to no advantage in gaining ulcer relief, and most people with ulcers continued to experience debilitating pain. Though stress reduction and dietary deductions hardly made any difference to patients, doctors continued to prescribe them as the best forms of ulcer treatment, blaming patients' inability to perfectly follow their low-stress/low-acid regimens for their continued suffering. However, an inquisitive doctor from Australia decided that discovering a true cure for ulcers required researchers to think outside of the realm of traditional medicine. He decided to experiment with ulcer tissue and explore its very nature. The results of his experiments were shocking.

After securing and analyzing ulcer biopsies from a number of patients, Dr. Barry Marshall discovered that all of the samples he had collected were colonized with a specific type of bacteria. Most doctors might have assumed that the bacteria were a logical consequence of the ulcers; longstanding stomach ulcer sores seem to be a prime breeding ground for germs. However, Dr. Marshall decided to examine the situation from the opposite perspective. He eventually discovered the bacteria were actually causing the ulcers by producing substances that damaged mucus-producing tissues and generated infection. Because the overwhelming majority of ulcer patients have been shown to exhibit the same bacteria, Dr. Marshall was able to devise an almost universal form of ulcer treatment consisting of a simple course of antibiotics. Because his curiosity inspired him to take a closer look at the ailment he was trying to treat, Dr. Marshall was able to cure thousands of people from a lifetime of pain while restoring their ability to enjoy active lifestyles and spicy food. The antibiotic cure continues to generate huge income and has won its innovator a Nobel Prize.

❧ ❧

The world's bacteria behave in strange ways, but the planet's creatures are even stranger. Earth is host to hundreds of thousands of fascinating species of animals, all of them surviving in their own unique (and sometimes bizarre) styles. Being curious about all types of life is not only a great way to understand more about the world around you, but it is also a great way to learn how to improve your own existence. Most folks don't question the idea that animals are helpful to innovation; we are all familiar with lab rats used to develop new medications and even cosmetics for human beings. However, the innovative underdog can learn from his other furry friends in a variety of other ways.

Consider the platypus, an animal that evokes the most extreme curiosity from most observers. The platypus is indeed a strange-looking mammal; its eclectic anatomy consists of a beaver tail, otter feet, and a duck bill, so that, simply put, the creature appears to have been assembled by a committee, from spare parts. One of the platypus's most unique features is its ability to excrete extremely toxic venom. Most scientists agree that the venom works as a way for the animal to defend itself against predators and establish dominance while mating. The solution is toxic enough to kill small animals such as dogs. It will not kill its human victims; however, the venom inflicts such intense pain that human sufferers might wish for their own demise anyway.

Unlike most mammals, whose venom systems are purely offensive in nature, the platypus's venom glands are defensive, having resulted from genes that were once involved in the immune system. Their venom consists of defensive proteins very similar to compounds that bolster immunity in other marsupials, such as koalas. Scientists are actively investigating the toxins in the platypus's venom that cause such agonizing pain. Once they figure out how and why the venom causes such adverse reactions, innovators will have the opportunity to design whole new classes of painkilling drugs without the addictive properties that many current pain-reducing drugs exhibit. Here's how: In order to find out how the venom causes pain, scientists must understand which of its chemicals stimulate which proteins in the human body. Once this information is obtained, scientists can engineer molecules capable of blocking all pain-causing agents from attacking those proteins.

The situation regarding the toxic chemicals and their targeted proteins is analogous to the relationships between keys and their corresponding locks. Suppose you discovered that the door to your home was capable of being unlocked by several different keys. In order to disable the lock so that none of those keys could access it, you would only have to discover one of the keys in question. By changing the lock to disallow just one key from opening it, you will have essentially made the lock inaccessible to all the keys that were once capable of accessing your residence. Similarly, in order to block all pain-causing agents, a scientist only has to change the "lock" on a human protein so that just one pain-causing chemical loses access. Every other toxic substance that was once capable of attacking that protein will no longer be effective either.

❧ ❧

Nature is an amazing source of medicines. Humanity has discovered a vast variety of natural cure throughout history, from quinine (an antimalarial that comes from the bark of the cinchona tree), to tamoxifen (a new drug for treating breast cancer that was discovered in the bark of the yew tree). Contrary to popular misconception, natural cures aren't just "healing potions" or remedies for minor ailments. Plants and animals are abounding with pharmaceuticals so potent that they can treat even modern day's most perplexing and serious diseases. It is quite possible that the cures for all cancers, and even devastating viruses such as HIV, are growing from the earth and swimming in the sea. And you don't have to be a seasoned scientist to discover them.

For instance, on today's market, there is a painkilling drug called Ziconotide that is derived from the venom of the cone snail *conus magnus*. Ziconotide is effectively used to manage the most intense levels of pain beyond the control of any other painkiller. Though it must be administered by direct injection into the spinal cord, Ziconotide works when nothing else does, without the addictive properties of other painkillers such as morphine. Interestingly enough, a young man discovered

Ziconotide when he was barely out of high school. Michael McIntosh was working as a lab technician under Dr. Baldomero Olivera when he stumbled upon the powerful painkiller residing in a tiny snail. His curiosity was likely fostered by Dr. Olivera, who dedicated his life to the study of animal toxins' impact on neuroscience after his childhood in the Philippines piqued his own curiosity about animal venom. Scientists are not yet sure why Ziconotide is so effective at blocking pain in humans, though they suspect that the drug blocks nerve channels in the spinal cord. However the drug works, the discovery of Ziconotide's true painkilling mechanisms is sure to bring even more effective drugs to the market. Similarly, discovering exactly why the cone snail developed this venom can enable scientists to seek out other organisms in possession of healing chemicals.

Venoms aren't the only animal secretions to become innovative gems for the curious underdog. Just about any substance an animal produces can be considered for medicinal purposes. For example, there are ancient marine organisms called hagfish that, though they have been around forever, are just now being appreciated for their innovative potential. Hagfish are most definitely ugly creatures. Their anatomy comprises the only animal makeup in existence that possesses a skull but no spinal column. Hagfish average about 18 inches long and they look similar to eels; however, this is where the resemblance ends. Unlike other slimy creatures, hagfish eat by slithering into the mouths of their prey and eating them alive from the inside out. Hagfish are even more unpleasant because they frequently secrete large quantities of noxious slime. The hagfish is scientifically notorious because its slime is actually viscoelastic (its stiffness is a direct function of the forces acting on it).

The slime's viscoelasticity enables it to essentially bounce between different states of matter depending on what substance it's released into. This means that when the hagfish secretes its mucus into an aquatic atmosphere, the thin and stringy slime becomes a thick and sticky mass under the water's pressure. The effect is so dramatic that an adult hagfish can produce enough slime to solidify a bucket of water in just seconds.

Scientists are not certain why hagfish developed this slime or why they continue to use it, but current theories indicate that the slime is a defense mechanism; in fact, it has been reported that sharks will break off an attack just seconds after first encountering a hagfish's slime. This is probably because the slime is difficult to penetrate and particularly foul-smelling; the substance is so offensive that even hagfish themselves detest it a great deal. In order to escape their own slimy secretions, hagfish have developed a remarkable way of freeing themselves from their messes: They tie themselves in a knot and literally pull themselves through it, scraping the slime off of their bodies as they go.

The physical nature of hagfish slime gets even more interesting. It is non-wetting, which means that if you stick your hand in a bucket of it, your digits will still be dry when you pull them out (though not particularly sweet-smelling). If you analyze the slime even one step further, you'll discover it boasts some fascinating chemical properties as well. For starters, if you freeze-dry it you will transform the mucus into a light, free-flowing powder. If you add water to the powder, you will restore it to its original slimy consistency, but only for an hour; after that, the substance will completely come apart and revert to a water-like viscosity. To many, the properties of hagfish slime might sound like a whole lot of useless information. However, those who have let themselves become curious about the fluid have come close to discovering some truly novel innovations.

One of those innovative opportunities involves taking hagfish slime from the deep sea to the battlefield. Obviously, soldiers in hot conflict zones tend to get hit with bullets that leave nasty holes in their bodies. Often, if the bullets themselves don't kill the soldiers they hit, the dirt and bacteria that enter the wounds will. As soon as a foreign agent or organism takes up house in a flesh wound, infection begins to escalate immediately. Therefore, the two prime concerns for medics treating bullet injuries are curtailing blood loss and preventing infection. Applying pressure and bandages might help somewhat to slow loss of blood, but the results of this treatment are half-desirable at best. Furthermore, bandaging wounds does very little to keep out bacteria. For this task, medics must apply some kind of antibacterial agent to the wound. However, both bandages and antibiotics together are not a perfect system, mainly because neither can effectively keep blood loss from killing the victim in seconds.

What happens when an innovator applies his or her curiosities about nature to a life-or-death issue? The answer to this question is beautifully illustrated in the future of hagfish slime. Recently, people have begun testing the substance's potential for saving soldiers' lives. In initial experiments, scientists have freeze-dried the slime and poured the resulting powder, along with some water, into a bullet wound. As soon as the powder makes contact with the right amount of water, the concoction swells up and completely seals the wound in seconds. After it's been put in place, the slime can effectively block bacteria from entering the wound and, if prepared with a suitable dry anticoagulant, can staunch the bleeding from even the most ragged injuries. Hagfish slime has not yet made the market as a first-aid essential; however, its use as an injury patch might make it one of the world's greatest innovations. Even more importantly, hagfish slime serves as a shining example of how being curious about the world around you is often the first step in the creative process.

❧ ❧

Many underdogs have never heard of the hagfish and its slime. But you don't have to be an expert in exotic marine life to discover innovative solutions from wildlife. There are many natural curiosities that are so well known that they've been accepted as mysterious anomalies instead of explored as potential problem-solvers. For instance, many people are familiar with the idea that, according to classical aerodynamic theory, honeybees should not be able to fly. The notion that honeybees should be incapable of flying is best traced back to 20th-century French scientists who calculated the "impossibility" using linear equations incorporating the honeybee's wing size and beats per minute. They concluded that honeybee wings are neither large enough, nor do they move quickly enough to propel bees into flight. Yet, despite calculations proving otherwise, honeybees seem to have no problem taking to the air. Science could have very well accepted that honeybees are somehow exceptions to aerodynamic rule and abandoned the pursuit to figure out exactly how they fly. However, simple curiosity drove scientists to plug away at the problem for more than 70 years. In the end, they not only explained one of nature's most baffling phenomena; they discovered a way to apply honeybee flight to a wide variety of human transportation vehicles.

Honeybees flap their tiny wings 240 times a second. Though this alone is not enough to lift them through the air, honeybees can take flight because they *rotate* their wings at the same time they flap them. This motion produces a vortex that literally sucks the honeybees into the sky. In order to understand the nature of this vortex, engineers had to develop a whole arsenal of cameras and instruments to capture honeybees' flying mechanisms in slow motion and measure their individual components precisely. Explaining how honeybees fly is not terribly important in itself (though, of course, it is always nice to know these things). What *is* important about this whole process is the fact that the information it's provided and the technology it's inspired can be applied to other situations. For instance, the cameras and instruments developed to measure the bees' motions are now being used to analyze other natural phenomena in incredibly detailed ways. Additionally, the mechanisms behind the honeybees' vortices are being applied to manmade aerial innovations in order to devise whole new classes of flying machines. Perhaps someday a revolutionary new type of airplane will make it possible to fly from Britain to Bangkok in 20 minutes, all because of the curiosity surrounding the simple honeybee.

❧ ❧

This chapter was designed to highlight some of the extraordinary curiosities of nature. Through years of investigation, the mechanisms behind some of nature's oddities have been explained and used in new innovations. However, there are many more mysteries left to be unraveled. Nature is a wonderful demonstrator of processes and materials far beyond our current level of knowledge. Just because we don't understand "why" something occurs does not mean we're excused from exploring the "what" itself.

Any underdog is capable of pursuing these natural mysteries. Think about the early South American Indians who, through a series of curiosity-driven experiments, discovered that a certain plant extracts contains poison so potent it could drop a target with just one dart-full. This extract is called curare, and it sparked the discovery of a whole range of muscle relaxants responsible for revolutionizing surgeries and treating a vast variety of debilitating neuromuscular diseases.

As an innovator, you should constantly look at the world around you and wonder, "Why?" Try to recall your own childhood curiosity, that incessant string of "Why, Mommy?" questions that once seemed to flow effortlessly from your mouth. Chances are that, as you became an adult, you were slowly dissuaded from asking so many curiosity-driven questions. Try your best to regain your youthful inquisitiveness; the thoughtful frame of mind is fun and rewarding.

Chapter 8

The Underdog Gets Mugged: Innovation Illustrated Through the Underdog's Favorite Brew

It's not unusual for underdogs to beg for a cup of coffee in the morning. There are very few hardworking people on this planet who don't find comfort in starting the day off right with a nice, rich, flavorful brew. In fact, the business of producing, distributing, and consuming coffee is so widespread that the beverage illustrates a wonderful range of innovations that has been ever-expanding for centuries. Each creative amendment to the way coffee is brewed and enjoyed is an outstanding achievement in itself. But most fascinating is how these innovations intertwine with and influence each other in extraordinary ways. Coffee isn't just a pick-me-up for the mind and body; its innovation history serves to stimulate the creative soul.

According to one popular legend, coffee was first discovered in the ninth century, when goat herders in the Ethiopian village of Choche discovered that their animals instantly pepped up after eating wild red Arabica coffee berries. Other lore suggests that coffee was not discovered until just 2,000 years ago in Yemen. Regardless of its exact origin, coffee's knack for carrying underdogs through their most difficult work is solidly stamped in history. Historians agree that slaves captured in the Sudan and sold in Yemen were able to keep up their strength by constantly consuming the outer flesh of coffee beans.

Around AD 500, history's first coffee houses opened for business in Cairo and Mecca. Coffee beans became an exclusive commodity in the Middle East; for a variety of reasons, the beans were not made available for export, so they could not be grown anywhere else on the map. Though these countries' coffee beans were closely guarded, their keepers weren't protecting much. Primitive Cairo coffee makers did not know to roast their beans before brewing them in a special vessel called an ibrik. As a result, the very first coffee houses were certainly no Starbucks—instead of frappacinos, they featured only thin, watery coffee with neither significant substance nor taste.

However, humans didn't easily abandon their ambition to perfectly utilize the coffee bean in beverage manufacturing. About a thousand years after "coffee water" made its debut, it was discovered that roasting and grinding up coffee beans before brewing them produced a much more satisfying beverage. It is not exactly clear what prompted the Yemenites to roast and grind their coffee beans, but this solution must have been more obvious to them than we might think. At the same point in history, the Egyptians were smashing flowers, berries, and roots in order to extract their fragrances for use in perfumes. Because innovation (in any era) is all about taking successful techniques from one industry and applying them to another, it makes sense that the people in Yemen would grind their beans as the Egyptians ground their flowers; doing this, both groups of people could extract maximum flavor from their goods.

❧ ❧

Let's fast forward a bit through coffee's history to Europe during the 1600s. At this point, coffee was (somewhat successfully) prepared by brewing roasted grounds in boiling water. The common conundrum, however, involved extracting the sandy grounds from the magical elixir before pouring it into a cup. There were a couple of solutions proposed and practiced to accomplish this task; however, both were significantly imperfect. Some coffee makers designed special spouts to trap the grounds in their pots; this allowed the liquid to pour forth freely. Other brew masters created pots with a lower compartment in which the grounds would settle (because they are heavier than water). Though both straining techniques sufficiently removed enough grounds to prevent coffee consumers from choking, neither came close to producing the ideal, smooth coffee beverage.

Though the common coffee brew was still a bit gritty, coffee drinking still flourished in popularity throughout Europe during the 17th century; the international passion reached a point where a group of English women actually banded together to make coffee drinking (and all related pastimes and establishments) illegal. Interestingly enough, the women's chief complaint was that their husbands were spending far too much time chitchatting in coffee houses and not enough hours fulfilling their responsibilities at home. As it stood, coffee was a wonderfully satisfying way to put pep in one's step while providing a common drink for conversation among friends. These qualities alone made coffee drinking more than worthwhile, but innovators around the world still worked tirelessly for hundreds of years to fulfill coffee's full potential as a hot, energizing, *and* delicious commodity.

By the 1780s, husbands had one more reason to avoid home: a revolutionary new coffee pot that filtered so finely that coffee became the desired taste of high society. The innovator of the groundbreaking brewer was a young man named George Biggin of Cosgrove, England. He had the brilliant idea to place a cloth sock across the top of a coffee pot to act as a filter. His pot's pouring spout was located beneath the sock, completely separated from the grounds, so that only coffee liquid poured forth from the pot. This first makeshift filter was certainly marked progress in history's coffee continuum; however, the quality of the coffee it could produce varied greatly, depending on how thoroughly the beans had been ground and how tightly the sock had been stitched. One should hope that the value of 18th-century coffee was not influenced by variables such as whether or not filter-socks had previously found homes of feet. Regardless, Europeans rejoiced over Biggin's boost to the coffee world.

❧ ❦

The French were fantastic contributors to coffee brewing. They initially achieved a coffee pot with two chambers stacked around a fine cloth filter—a subtle improvement to the English sock system. Eventually they developed a metal filter that worked with much more efficiently than cloth. In true innovative spirit, the French also realized that improving the business of coffee meant breaking out of the box and considering the problem from all angles. Finding better filtering wasn't the only way a person could go about innovating the coffee experience. After considering the existing science behind brewing a particularly good pot of joe, the French honed in on the fact that the temperature at which coffee is brewed makes a significant difference in its flavor. To capitalize on this principle, they engineered a way to keep water from cooling down during the slow brewing and filtering process: a type of insulating jacket that fit around a coffee pot and encased its water content in a heat-sustaining space.

As time progressed, people came up with even more ways to revolutionize coffee production. Louis Bernard Babaut developed an original espresso machine that brewed by forcing steam through coffee grounds. Madame Vassieux improved this design by creating what was known as the "vacuum pot." This device required that water boil and generate enough steam to saturate the coffee grounds. When the water was removed from its heat source, it underwent a cooling process by which the reduction in temperature created a natural vacuum. The suction effect pulled the condensed coffee steam down into a lower-level chamber where it collected to form a liquid brew.

As time marched on, the first percolator was developed. The percolating pot consisted of an upper chamber to hold coffee grounds and a lower chamber to hold water. A metal tube that ran between the two compartments enabled boiling water to bubble up through the grounds and then drip back down into the lower chamber. Though this technique worked wonders to keep the grounds separated from the drink, it was not without fault. In order for the water to raise and bubble appropriately, it had to be heated to a boil. However, it was soon discovered that boiling water produced bitter coffee. Here, the French (always concerned with creating quality coffee) crafted an elegant alternative to the problematic percolator: the French press. The French press is what truly captured all the components of successful coffee brewing in one machine. Its chief innovative mechanism was a physical plunger that worked to separate grounds from coffee once brewing was complete. It provided efficient means to produce a smooth, grounds-free brew, uncorrupted by the bitter taste associated with boiling water.

Even though the French press nearly perfected the taste and texture of the common brew, coffee connoisseurs were hardly satisfied. Because coffee could now be appreciated by purely the palate, consumers were less and less impressed by coffee's caffeine content. So that coffee could be enjoyed in the evening (and by people with adverse reactions to caffeine), coffee innovators began to develop a drink possessing all the coffee flavor without any of the "hype." Eventually, the demand for a more mellow mix was met and, in 1903, the coffee-loving world was introduced to Sanka coffee, the brew that was literally "sans caffeine."

❧ ❦

Once coffee became a smooth, non-bitter brew, and it could be served up from breakfast to after dinner, innovators found a way to link coffee making with convenient cleanup. In 1912, a German housewife named Melitta Benz innovated a disposable coffee filter constructed from blotting paper. The device replaced multiple-use cloth filters, which were much more expensive to purchase and took significantly more time to clean. Instead of having to soak and scrub a cloth filter after each pot it produced, homemakers such as Melitta could now simply crumple a used paper filter into a ball and effortlessly toss it into the trash.

Soon after the advent of the disposable coffe filter, coffee became even more drinker-friendly. In 1938, coffee innovators produced a freeze-dried coffee named

Nescafe. By 1963, the Bunn Corporation had commercialized a coffeemaker that simultaneously heated water, brewed coffee, and kept its contents warm on a convenient, heated plate. The advent of such technology paved the way for Starbucks to open its first location in Seattle in 1971. Because coffee boasts such an expansive history of powerful innovations, its producers continue to enjoy its booming business. Today, a great variety of new coffee franchises have risen to immense popularity. Up-and-coming coffee companies continue to innovate enough new brews and business models to seriously challenge Starbucks' domination of the industry. This situation is a beautiful illustration of how innovation is continuously driven by underdogs.

⋇⋇

So many underdogs take their morning cups of joe for granted that few of them appreciate what coffee can teach us about innovation. Considering its progression from bitter water to a bold, rich, bountiful beverage, it is important to recognize what coffee represents in the world of creativity. For starters, the drink illustrates how a series of seemingly simple innovations and discoveries can work together to create a worldwide industry. Once only used to feed energy to slaves, coffee is now consumed by the entire world in more than 7 million tons each year. And just because it's become so popular doesn't mean that coffee has reached its creative peak. Today there is ever-increasing demand for more coffee that is more efficiently grown and more easily purchased. Fortunately, there is also increasing incentive to fairly compensate coffee growers while ensuring that they use the most ecologically friendly methods of cultivating their crops.

You might think that coffee innovations have little more purpose than improving the quality and quantity of café items. However, creating better coffee isn't just about creating more sophisticated products and processes; it's about promoting fairness and protecting the people who make the coffee trade possible at all. One of the most important innovations in coffee's history has nothing to do with its texture or flavor: Instead, it illustrates a truly novel way to improve the lives of people working at the bottom of an industry pyramid. And this innovation was entirely orchestrated by underdogs.

Columbian coffee growers have fought a long-standing battle against the falling coffee prices that often devastated their standard of living. Because the growers cannot possibly perfect their coffee beans any more than they already have, improving their product is no way to guarantee more stable sales in a market full of fluctuations. However, in 1927, a group of growers got together with a brilliant plan to protect their lives and their livelihoods. They formed the National Federation of Coffee Growers of Colombia, a group that works to stabilize the Columbian coffee market while ensuring its independent farmers have access to all the essentials of life.

The federation is nonprofit and nonpolitical; it is funded by taxes collected from coffee exports, and overseen by the Columbian government. Ordinarily, falling coffee prices would harshly affect the average Columbian coffee grower, jeopardizing his ability to pay for his business's tools and supplies, his children's education, and even his family's food and utilities. But with the federation in place, farmers are protected from falling coffee prices at the same time they are privileged to sell their coffee on the open market. When coffee prices fall below minimum, the federation intervenes and buys the crop, storing it to sell on the world market in times of shortage. This arrangement guarantees farmers steady income for their work while protecting their right to sell their crops even when prices rise above the federation minimum. Because its numbers are so strong, the federation is able to finance a whole range of social projects and programs, from the building of access roads to the maintenance of a safe water supply to the guarantee of electric, housing, healthcare, and education. Even more impressive, the federation also offers coffee growers low-cost loans and training in new methods of producing the highest-quality crops.

Though the federation itself is a huge, innovative feat, its organizers have come up with an even more unique way to give Columbian coffee a best-selling brand identity. "Juan Valdez" is the fictitious farmer who's become the iconoclastic image emblazoned on every Columbian coffee product you've undoubtedly ever seen. His face is not only the logo of the world's most cherished brand of coffee, but it is also the symbol of the hardworking underdog who grows and harvests a true, quality product. All in all, the National Federation of Coffee Growers of Colombia represents a stunning innovation in transforming the world of coffee from a small, fragmented industry to a huge, standardized national business with a great sense of social responsibility. The arrangement serves both the producers and the consumers of the coffee bean: Coffee farmers are free to harvest their crops without risk to their fragile livelihood, and coffee customers are delighted to continuously buy from a brand they trust.

❧ ❦

The coffee industry exemplifies how innovations build upon each other to create empires. It also demonstrates how innovations do more than just make customers' lives easier; a truly developed field of innovation

125

serves underdogs on both sides of the consumer equation. But there is at least one more truly wonderful way coffee teaches innovators to think out of the box.

Innovation is truly an art. Therefore, many of the principles of innovation correlate to the principles of design. When an artist composes a design, he or she works to create a pattern that is balanced in both color and shape. Though most people only notice the elements at the forefront of an artist's work, the background, or negative space, plays just as important a role in establishing an aesthetically pleasing piece. In the same way that artists use the positive and negative (painted and empty) parts of their canvases, innovators should strive to use both the positive and negative components of their materials. In the case of coffee, it seems that most innovators have primarily been concerned with the coffee bean's "positive" part: the component of the berries that is readily transformed into that now-famous beverage. However, the part of the coffee bean that stars at Starbucks is only a tiny percentage of the bean's entire weight. Coffee innovators spent centuries trying to filter out coffee grounds from their coffee cups, believing that the grounds were essentially waste. However, this "negative," or background part of the coffee bean is just as important as the part that makes the coffee beverage. Currently, almost 7 million tons of grounds have been produced by coffee makers all over the world. To coffee brewers, these grounds might be trash, but to innovators, they're tremendous treasure.

It turns out that coffee "waste" is as useful and will become as popular as the coffee drink itself. Grounds have a variety of uses that work from the "ground" up. Most commonly, coffee grounds are used as soil additives; their light, airy texture is the perfect contrast to the density of clay soils. By combining used coffee grounds with heavy dirt, planters can improve the quality of their soil and give their crops more room to breathe and even more nutrients. There are other benefits to using coffee grounds in gardens: They work as fantastic ant repellents. Just a small sprinkle of grounds around your cherished tomato plants is more than enough to make that string of ants march elsewhere. Snails and slugs are also motivated to move away from plants when coffee grounds are present. In effect, coffee grounds are the gardener's Miracle-Gro, functioning to give plants an oxygen-rich, nutrient-fortified, and pest-free place to flourish for little money and hardly any time.

Coffee grounds also make excellent fueling material; when burned, they produce higher heat levels and release less atmospheric pollutants than even sawdust. Innovators at one of Nestlé's plants in the Philippines have actually devised a way to turn leftover grounds, collected from producing instant coffee, into fuel. By using one of its waste products to provide energy, this Nestlé plant is able to save more than 4,000 tons of oil, reduce its acid rain emissions by nearly 300 tons, and eliminate 70,000 tons of landfill-bound waste each year.

Ironically, the grounds that coffee innovators worked so hard to prevent from polluting their smooth coffee concoctions are actually great water purifiers. Some scientists in New Zealand have shown that coffee grounds are tremendously effective in removing toxic, heavy metals from drinking water. Their experiments have shown that, once coffee grounds have been allowed to absorb metals from water, they can be filtered out and actually separated from the metal they've collected. The metals can then be used accordingly to suit a variety of other purposes, and the coffee grounds can be put to the purification process again.

❧ ❧

Coffee grounds are also capable of purifying water in another way. Recently, an Australian innovator named Tony Flynn developed a brilliant method of using coffee grounds to cheaply and effectively remove even the smallest, most harmful microbes from water. His recipe for bringing fresh water to the poor of the Third World is simple: Only a small mound of clay, a cup of recycled coffee grounds, and a bit of good old fashioned cow manure are needed to generate sparkling clean water. Flynn's filter can be made easily, by anyone, living just about anywhere. The device is constructed from a handful of crushed clay mixed with coffee grounds and saturated with enough water to give the blend the consistency of a stiff biscuit mix. The concoction is then shaped as a cylindrical pot and allowed to dry in the sun. Then the pot is cooked within a halo of straw and burning cow manure; these two materials generate enough heat so that the pot can be baked without a kiln. The firing process solidifies the clay and burns away the coffee grounds so that the result is a pot containing pores that are large enough to accommodate water but small enough to trap and remove common pathogens such as E. coli. Flynn's pot can filter a liter of water to a level of 99-percent purity within just two hours while costing almost nothing to operate.

The World Health Organization estimates that more than 80 percent of all illness is due to unsafe water. Especially in Third World nations, children under the age of 5 annually suffer approximately 1.5 billion bouts of diarrhea, of which almost 4 million are fatal. Tony Flynn's water filter (the result of simply creative thought and coffee beans) has the potential to almost completely reverse these staggering figures. His creation is proof that innovations aren't only about exploring new materials and technology. Sometimes the most imperative, life-saving ideas stem from the desire to use up old materials to get them out of the way.

❧ ❧

The simple fact is that innovations don't just spring from our most attractive and appealing sources and surroundings. Some of the world's best discoveries have sprung from materials that don't look so beautiful, smell very great, or taste too delightful. Quite often, innovators can become so wrapped up in how materials appeal to their senses that they let this superficial information blind them to substances' true usefulness. This is most likely the reason why one of the world's most effective and basic means of purifying water wasn't innovated until the 21st century. As a world-class innovator, you must be able find the treasure abounding in materials other people treat as trash.

In order to achieve this level of understanding, it helps to reflect on where the concept of the "diamond in the rough" comes from. Consider the diamond itself, the world's most precious gemstone. When most people conjure up the idea of white ice, they envision a picture of flawless perfection. Indeed, diamonds are sold according to standards of pristine cut, color, and clarity. The more precise the cut, the more sparkling white the color, the more crystal clear, the more a diamond is capable of making jaws drop and heads turn. Although it is true that the price of a diamond increases considerably with the size of its carat weight, the real value of a diamond rests in its possession of perfect clarity. Yet diamonds hardly grow from such perfection at all.

Diamonds are a girl's best friend, but the bond between the girl and her gemstone might suffer a bit if she knew exactly where her precious beauty came from. Diamonds are actually found in the ground where they must first grow for millions of years in very dirty, bacteria-laden volcanic lava. If diamonds didn't spend so much time in the muck, they would never experience the right conditions needed to become such items of great value and beauty. Diamonds are just one example of perfection that grows from a complete mess. There are even comparable matters existing in the realm of human health. For instance, a study from Great Britain shows that there is a direct correlation between socio-economic status and incidence of asthma. The wealthier a family is, the more likely its children will be taken care of by a private nanny instead of a daycare infested with childhood diseases. However, early exposure to such ailments is what develops a strong, healthy immune system, the type of protection needed against such chronic conditions as asthma. Without germs, there cannot be complete health; likewise, without the use of "waste"—including coffee grounds—certain life-giving innovations cannot exist. Coffee teaches us that even inferior-tasting, -smelling, and -appearing substances are capable of creating perfection.

Chapter 9

Financing a Venture: How the Underdog Digs for Dollars

A common complaint of would-be innovators is that their creativity is held captive by their lack of resources. The problem with this idea is that many people use it as an excuse to stop innovating before they even start. Most people bemoan their lack of resources prematurely—that is, before they even have an innovation that requires resources in the first place. An overwhelming percentage of people who make a big issue over not enough sources and supplies are underdogs who have actually trained their brains to resist creatively until, somehow, miraculously, an exorbitant amount of money lands in their pockets and cuts the leash. This is not hard to see happening.

The truth is that resources come in many shapes, sizes, and colors. And not all of them are flat, rectangular, and green. Very few people, including those who have contributed the world's most celebrated innovations, have extra money to take that great idea from their under-ground, basement laboratories to the center stage of the consumer market. Of course, most innovations will ulti-mately require substantial investment dollars before the innovator sees serious profitability. However, there are many preliminary steps to be taken in the innovative process before any money must be raised at all. The dif-ference between a commercially successful innovation and one that dies, unfulfilled, is an innovator's ability to use time and people as resources for fetching financial provisions.

Whether we like it or not, nothing in this world, not even an idea, is free. Many of us know that time, though it's not typically associated with the gold standard, is actually the most expensive and valuable resource we can ever invest in our own ideas. Time is such a crucial venture in your innovation because it is the only cur-rency that can shape and perfect your idea. Though spending time on your idea works at the expense of us-ing that time elsewhere to make more money, time is a resource anyone can make available—if only one is willing to completely believe in an innovation.

⋈ ⋊

Money fits into most peoples' lives under one of three categories: money earned, money not earned, and money spent. Many underdogs are too timid to ever think of lifting their lives from category one, but innovations al-ways require some kind of personal investment. Because the first funds to be transferred to your idea should be from your time, you should expect to move your posi-tion from category one to category two very near the beginning of the innovative process. After a bit of time, most innovators will usually find themselves straddling the fence between categories two and three, between investing time and contributing cold hard cash, as they build up their ventures. It is important to keep in mind that money spent correctly will ultimately convert into money made. When you enter into category three, and start putting money where your time can't take you, the most important way to use your dollars is to establish a powerful, loyal, and hardworking company team.

No matter how much of your money filters through each category, you must always keep your funds in one general, super class: money prioritized. Even if your innovation is as seemingly simple as a new way to crack eggs, you better be prepared to invest a lot of time and money into cracking a serious quantity of shells. The sooner you can be honest with yourself that the eggs will never be free (whether you buy them from a friendly farmer or invest in raising your own chickens), the better off you'll be. Even if you vow to utilize your innovative waste in your household's daily diet, eating egg salad, egg scrambles, and eggnog won't negate the costly time you'll have to spend "cracking the code" (and chances are your cholesterol-laden diet will create chaos for your arteries, a sure financial heartbreak for you and your insurance company later).

A good rule of thumb to follow when crossing over into category three, money spent, is that you should make company recruitment the heart of your investment. Once you've discovered a brilliant new way to make an omelet, a great way to use your money is to develop a prototype to show off that idea. And the first place you'll want to look for an audience isn't at a national food show. Before you look for customers, you have to form a company—even if that company consists of only you at the start. Of course, your ultimate goal will be to acquire a fully functional team. But even before you have a company staff, you must actually form a company. When your venture is recognized legally as a company, you'll be able to obtain extra protection for your endeavors, and you will appear more professional and secure to potential investors. Do not panic at the thought of becoming a one-man company; it is much easier to attract team members to an established company than to an unofficial group. In the meantime, remember that one person can wear many hats.

❧ ❦

Business development is even more dependent on people than it is on dollars. Because the majority of your marketing money will come from investors, the people you put behind your business propositions are absolutely key to your company's success. There are many breeds of business builders—developers, sales representatives, financial experts, legal assistants, and administrators—and each one is as unique and vital to your innovation as the others; all of these people will help you procure the most important people of all: your investors. So that you might get acquainted with the biology of the complex company organism, the following will briefly discuss the types of people you will want to have in your company's team, and how they should work together to bring in even the most difficult investor.

You will first find yourself in need of a strong business developer, a person who will essentially function as the strong (and hopefully flexible) glue that holds your company together in one piece. Business developers are responsible for figuring out how big your business should be at any given time. They are also in charge of talking to customers to find out what kind of people will pay what kind of money for what kind of product. Marketing your genius egg-cracking innovation? If you've got a great business developer, he or she will visit the kitchens of all kinds of folks to assess the value, efficiency, and appeal of your product.

Business developers should adhere themselves to the seams between all parts of a company. They should constantly work with the finance and marketing departments to determine the appropriate amount of advertisement, entertainment, and travel dollars that should be put into the promotion of your product. A business developer should work according to his or her title—development is an ongoing process that should never stagnate; thus, the business developer should be in constant communication with your customers and your company. Your company's glue should never dry out, and so your developer's duties should never diminish. A company should always prepare to grow larger and make changes to its innovations in order to better suit the appropriate markets. Eggshells might not change at all within the next couple of centuries, but your innovative egg cracker might be discovered for an infinite amount of other uses or constructed with an unlimited quantity of new materials. Keeping your company alive means exercising it constantly in the consumer world, while keeping it fresh and new. Your business developer should function as your company's personal trainer. Accept no less.

The next people on your company's roster should be your sales representatives. A lot of new business owners are not overly enthusiastic about adding salespeople to their company's team. This is probably because most people envision salespeople in a purely retail environment. A pet peeve shared more universally than most is the pushy, relentless sales clerk who pops up out of nowhere, never seems to go away, and is only capable of offering little help in the way of useless formality: "Can I ask you how you are today (even though I'm not really interested)? Can I help you find your size (even though you probably know your pants size better than your phone number)?" But company salespeople are really nothing of the sort; they are absolutely critical to the success of your innovation because they seek out customers who are truly interested in your product and need some vital questions answered. Your sales team's ideas should abound with creative ways to install your innovation into the lives of as many people as possible. In the Middle Ages, salespeople resorted to such tactics as kidnapping entire families until their patriarchs paid for an oustanding order, but today's sales practices are a lot less desperate and disagreeable.

It is important to remember that people are hesitant to buy innovations for the same reasons they are hesitant to create them: People are skeptical of the power of innovation. This is why it is so important for your company to have sales representation; educating potential customers about your product and/or service makes a huge difference in whether or not they'll buy it. Unfortunately, human nature is such that people must be thoroughly convinced the world can be a better, easier, and more efficient place before they'll believe that life doesn't have to be terribly difficult. This shift in perspective is accomplished with an honest and effective sales pitch. Don't worry if your company is a small start-up venture without the immediate funds for a sales department. As the founder of your company, you are your own most highly qualified sales representative, the person most able to amend your product/service to meet your customers' demands. However, when your company has expanded to the point at which your attention is needed elsewhere, you'll want to concentrate on hiring a sales team to do the product pitching for you.

It is an interesting irony that some of a company's most essential contributors are also its most laughed about. Some of these picked-upon souls are the financial folk of the word. Financial advisors have gotten a bad rap throughout the years for the precise quality that makes them incredibly useful in the first place: their almost obsessive attention to detail. Of course, there exists the well-recognized stereotype of the dour, compulsive financial guy who takes a special delight in insisting on a receipt for that 10-cent tip you left on a cup of coffee a year ago. But if your financial person has tabs on every cup of joe you drink, you can bet he's completely fixated on keeping the squeaky-clean tax papers that will save your company the anguish of ever having to deal with the IRS. Having a financial person in your company is not negotiable, no matter how small your business initially is. Even if your financial department is at first just an extra-scrupulous bookkeeper, paid by the hour, you're better off safe than sorry.

Lawyers just might be the only professionals out there who suffer more jokes than financial gurus. In fact, there are probably more bits of humor about the profession than actual attorneys, past, present, and future. Yet, in my own innovative career, I've been most captivated by the kind of comedy that pokes fun, not at attorneys, but at the people who fail to hire them. There is a classic cartoon that wonderfully demonstrates what can happen when an attorney isn't part of a company team. The illustration shows a very confounded salesperson on the phone with a frantic product development guy; the latter is screaming, "You promised them a WHAT? WHEN?" When you are selling your innovation, you are contractually bound, either explicitly or implicitly, to standards and expectations regarding what your product must deliver. To put it simply, what you sell has to work, and if it doesn't, you need backup.

Even if your product works flawlessly every time, even if your revolutionary egg cracker breaks a shell sans effort *and* mess without fail, you still need legal protection. There are many crazy customers out there, and sometimes their expectations will be ridiculous. Years ago, a woman sued McDonald's because she expected her coffee to be hot to the taste but cool to the touch when the cup she straddled between her legs in her car spilled over the lid and scorched her. You might find that one of your egg-cracker customers bought your innovation with the expectation that the device not only removes the contents of an egg from its shell, but also separates the yolks from the whites, cooks its own omelet, and cleans up the kitchen afterward. This example is obviously exaggerated, but not to such a degree that it bears no resemblance to scenarios you might encounter that are almost as silly (and scary).

The last link in your company's chain should be your administrative workers. These are the people who act as lubricant on all the parts of a business that might become rusty or misaligned. In my experience, the most important person in any company is the office manager, because he or she is trained to be the lifeline of every other part of the workforce. Underdogs don't live in offices and laboratories; innovators come from all walks of life, and most of them have other jobs and families outside of their pet projects. This is why the underdog's company needs an office manager, the go-to guy or gal who knows where everyone is and where everything is kept, and can cover for you when you're at your child's school play or you have a particularly difficult customer on the phone.

❧ ❧

So what do you do once you've rounded up and integrated an expert group of people into your company? When you have your company's development, sales, financial, and legal departments all up and running together, your next immediate step is to pull everyone's expertise together and pitch your product to investors. Garnering investment dollars is the only way most people are ever able to get their innovations moving in the market (and pay their company members; salaries). Seeking out and securing investments can be tricky business, and holding an investment meeting with your brand-new company for the first time can prove to be difficult and unfamiliar ground to tread.

The following is just a brief example of dialog that can be expected when company members get together to pitch themselves to a potential investor. Note that some company members' motivations might prove unacceptable to the way you would want to have your business run. Take note of some of the undesirable psychology you will want to prevent in your workers.

Patricia (Chief Executive Officer): "Good morning, everyone. Today we are going to review our cash position, work out a budget, and then get ready for our meeting with the investor."

Patricia is setting the company agenda by calling attention to items that are of specific concern to investors. These are the tasks at hand, but the implicit plan of action is to make each company characteristic look as optimistic and enticing as possible so that the investor might be persuaded to invest more money at an ever-higher valuation. Though focusing on your company's presentation is ever important, make sure that the substance of your business is enough to carry the exterior image you present to you investors; Patricia should possess more than enough information to back up any claims she makes.

Clark (Chief Financial Officer): "For my part, I can attest that we have enough money in the bank to continue to pay salaries for another six weeks, assuming that we can stall our creditors a little longer."

Clark wants the company to look as if it has its financial act together, but he may have already pulled a few moves in order to squeeze the life out of money the company doesn't have. Clark is amazingly talented at not returning phone calls except from people who owe the company money. He is able to proclaim, "Check is in the mail!" with a completely straight face and a tone of upright sincerity. Be careful to remember that the Clarks of your company should be policy-enforcers, not policy-makers; a higher authority should make certain that the financial folks don't cross lines and cut corners where they shouldn't.

Bob (Vice President of Sales): "I have fantastic news for you all. Our sales pipeline looks great, and we have several new hot prospects. If we close all those prospective deals this quarter at their projected sizes, we won't need to worry about any external financing."

Bob is trying mightily to get his fellow teammates in a positive frame of mind for the investment meeting, but he is risking his credibility big time by running away with sweeping, inaccurate fantasies. Sales never close with 100-percent certainty and at maximum value by the end of a given quarter. And because acquiring outside investments should always be the goal of a start-up company, rallying the crew to feel that it can work even without investments could lead to an overconfident overstep capable of ruining any financial investment.

Andrew (Vice President of Corporate Plans): "We're right on track for a merger with Acquirer's International."

Company owner beware: Andrew's definitive statement could be coupled with an uncertain fine print, something along the lines of: "Of course International will want to see our financial records and our forecasts, and whatever isn't up to par can be sugarcoated and wrapped in stacks of paper so thick that International will have neither the time nor desire to go through it all."

Be wary of company members who try to hide too many rusty needles in your company's haystack. Although investors usually want to hear nothing but good news and get upset when they don't, they are also apt to realize when a company's situation is being spun around so that things seem better than they are. If your company appears too good to be true, too put together for a start-up venture without existing assets, investors won't be shy about probing more deeply to uncover the ugly stuff. When it comes time to decide what you should disclose to your investors and what is in your best interests to keep behind closed doors, a good policy is to treat your openness as a function of your relationship with your investor. Complete honesty about your product, your financial situation, and your customer relations is usually absolutely necessary, but, when you are dealing with a somewhat less sophisticated investor, some company details should not be highlighted (though they should never be completely hidden or denied).

For example, I once employed a VP of engineering who turned out to be not quite right for the job; he was a very nice man, but he was somewhat in the wrong spot at the wrong time. I knew it was in the company's best interests for him to be replaced at the soonest possible opportunity, but I didn't have the resources to keep him and hire a replacement to work in tandem for several months. So I had to keep the engineer on board until I was able to bring in someone else more appropriate. Such is an issue one would be wise not to share with an investor, because a product is only a part of what attracts investors; they want to put their confidence in a fully functioning management team. In this situation, I knew sharing the details of my minor engineering employee snafu might scare my investors off, even though the integrity of my company was still very much intact. Therefore, I waited until the deal came through to make a move, and, with the company's new funds, I brought in the right man for the job and the company moved forward smoothly.

Sam (Vice President of Engineering): "Well, gentlemen, I believe we have every reason to feel confident in the product even though we have a few trouble spots. Since these features are fixable, we need not bother the investor with the details."

When you're managing your company's procedures, especially its product pitches, you must be on the lookout for imaginative innovations to the English language. Many people in all departments will come up with some creative ways to adjust what they're saying so that the product's predicament seems a lot easier to swallow. In this instance, Sam from engineering decided that referring to product glitches as "features" would be a safe way to disguise some serious technical issues and avoid dealing with the potential problems they might cause for consumers.

Labeling an innovation's deficiencies as "features" goes one step further in trying to deceive the people putting money into your company (your investors) and the people putting money into your product (your customers). In effect, this semantic game tries to advertise a flaw as a plus instead of a minus. If, for instance, your egg cracker has the tendency to slip from the shell and smash a few fingers, you wouldn't want your company to publicize your product's "bone-crushing strength" in order to secure a couple thousand more sales. Preparing to meet with an investor should be taken as seriously as the steps taken to sell your product to customers; be careful to make sure no fallacies get indoctrinated into your investment, marketing, and sales pitches.

Garrett (Vice President and General Counsel): "In order to get ourselves familiarized with our prospective investor, I am going to circulate the latest draft of our investment term sheet. If you have any complaints or corrections, please get back to me as soon as possible."

Garrett is probably praying to himself that none of the underdogs at the start-up company are making any representations to friends and family about the present state and future outlook of the company. The Securities and Exchange Commission, which enforces the integrity of investments and stock issuances, gets very upset with start-ups that raise funds without appropriate disclosures and caveats. But Garrett, and especially the owner of the company, should forgo silent prayers in favor of being profoundly explicit about the company's critical commitment to play by the rules.

Patricia: "Before we depart, I need to know how much money another 18 months of operations will cost us. As you all well know, fundraising has been a massive time investment, and it distracts me from my other, more important, responsibilities."

Patricia raises an essential question about fundraising here: Although her lack of enthusiasm is a bit of a concern, it is important for the company to determine how much fundraising is enough.

Acquiring investments is a balancing act. The idea is that your venture should bring in as much money as possible without requiring you to give up too much of your ownership. This is a scenario in which you can definitely have too much of a good thing; if you raise too much money, you will actually hurt yourself by diluting your ownership in a pool too deep with different investors. However, if you don't raise enough money, you will have wasted money in the process, and you will have to redirect and redo your efforts. Worse, you will have to answer accusations that you, either dishonestly or ineptly, didn't correctly estimate your company's needs and revenues the first time. If you are forced to undertake another round of fundraising, investors might see your company as even worse off than before, and your next attempt to find funds may be at a lower valuation (a down round).

The previous conversation illustrates the most common pitfalls that threaten start-up companies, as well as the shortcuts and missteps such ventures can make if all of their parts (people) do not function together integrally. If your company isn't itself working optimally, it won't work to bring in investments, because investors are quite particular people. If you compare all the people in your start-up company to a group of ambitious underdogs, you might want to extend the analogy and liken your investor to a finicky feline. As much as the lovable underdog, the humble and down-to-earth start-up, thinks that his investors are his friends, they really aren't, no matter how many dog treats he shares with them. Investors are not filled with benevolent interests; they will invest in your company in order to make more money, more quickly than they might in the stock market. Investors might smile a lot and gush about how happy they are to be on board your company's ship, but, if that ship starts to sink, you have to be prepared for their claws to come out—big time.

❧ ❧

The following is what will likely take place once your company has its act together and is ready to ask for funds.

Antoinette (CEO of CIT Investments): "Good morning, everyone. I sure hope that things have not gone to the dogs since we last talked. I've read over your business plan and have a considerable number of questions."

Antoinette has started the meeting off in pretty typical investor fashion; she's prepared to make you work for your money. Investors often think extremely highly of themselves; they believe they hold the cards because they source the money. To a degree, they are unfortunately correct in thinking that you need them more than they need you.

Antoinette: "It is important for me to first ask you all what you feel are your company's greatest strengths."

Here, Antoinette is setting a high-end expectation for the group to fill. If the company is too modest here, it will detrimentally put a cap on how much money it can pull in from the investor. The rule of thumb here is pretty inherent to asking for any type of money: You can be certain you will never get more than you asked for, only less.

Patricia: "Well, our company has a great deal of strengths, but particularly notable are our extremely experienced management team, our strong sales pipeline, and our superior product."

This is a pretty standard response and it is more or less not very interesting to the investor, because it is cut and pasted from just about every investor/start-up meeting the world has ever seen. Your investor is much more concerned about what is wrong with your company than what is right.

Antoinette: "What about your weaknesses?"

This is where the investor's ears will perk up as she delights in bringing the underdogs back to fiscal reality. Your investor will likely treat your proposition as an overambitious request, but this does not mean that you actually did ask for too much money and that you shouldn't stand your ground.

Patricia: "Our competition has been very successful. They have raised a lot of money and have a lot more people on their staff. Their bloat, however, is exactly why we will catch up to them, soon."

Patricia did the skillful thing in this situation by drawing on another company's positive as her company's negative instead of digging up a negative inherent in her company alone. And because she has a legitimate point, the investor is likely to give her answer a considerable amount of respect.

Antoinette: "That's wonderful; may I see a demonstration of your product?"

If your company is marketing egg crackers, you should be prepared to serve a personally prepared omelet for each investor at your table. Having a prototype of your innovation to support your request for financing is an absolute must; sketches, charts, and purely hypothetic ideas are never enough to satisfy an investor who is just dying to find something wrong with your company's presentation.

Antoinette (wiping the corners of her mouth): "Well, the egg cracker seems to have functioned, in this instance, very well. But what do you think about finding a way to produce egg shells that don't need to be cracked at all: soft shells that effortlessly peel away from the center?"

Antoinette is demonstrating that just because the product worked doesn't mean she's impressed. She is trying to fluster the company's presenter by pointing out the fact that she can't innovate a way to walk on water. Her comments also invite management to prove that they can think on their feet.

Patricia: "That sounds like a terrific idea; however, we are a kitchen appliance business and not a genetic engineering company. Our knowledge of agriculture is deliberately limited because trying to innovate a new type of egg shell would ruin the need for our original creation."

Just because someone has capital and has entertained the demonstration of your product does not mean he or she understands what your idea is all about. If all the investor has is money, and she isn't capable of

147

> *making intellectual or strategic contributions to the*
> *company, she isn't worth sharing in ownership of your*
> *idea. If her obstinacy persists, it's best to go someplace*
> *else for financing.*

After the demonstration is over, Antoinette has two choices regarding her possible investment: She can choose to walk away, or she can make a starting proposal (a starting proposal is usually insultingly low).

If Antoinette decides to walk away, you'll probably hear something along these lines: "Overall, the egg cracker is impressive indeed, but I will have to take what I've seen today and talk it over with my partners. We have to make sure that our investment portfolio is balanced before we take on any new ventures. We also must check your references."

Chances are, this means Antoinette is a vegetarian and she couldn't care less about financing the egg cracker. She might check your references for the fun of it, but, unless one of them claims your product can heal the sick and raise the dead, you'll probably get a call a week or two later with a big "thanks but no thanks." Getting turned down by an investor isn't a tragedy; there are plenty of people with money to put in your pot—you just have to discover the good eggs.

An investor's interest in your company might be even less encouraging than his or her rejection. Maybe Antoinette skipped breakfast the morning of your meeting, and the speed at which your egg cracker eased her aching belly compelled her to make an offer. But even if your innovation and the way you present it are both brilliant, you're only likely to hear something as enthusiastic as this: "I like it. Of course, the product does contain some 'warts' (negative features) that will bring its value down. Therefore, in exchange for the money you're asking for, we will need 65-percent equity and two seats on your board in order to make the investment." In this case, you're probably dealing with someone who wants to make a deal for cheap. With this much control of the business, your investors would be able to do whatever they like with your company; they could even sell it to someone else in order to make their cash profit sooner. You have a bit of maneuvering room in this situation, but you're only likely be able to talk your potential investor down somewhat.

❧ ❧

It's important to realize that start-up companies do much better with (well-matched) investors than they would alone, but, if you are to strike a fair deal that won't leave you out of control of your own company, you have to know that you don't *need* investors at all. If you cannot stomach prospective investment offers, you always have the option of taking out bank loans to finance your venture. Bank loans are expensive, and most must be guaranteed with personal assets, so if your egg cracker really does crack knuckles, it's likely you'll have to repay your bank loan with your house and car. A good idea is to treat investors as a tool for developing a strong and successful company. Before you find yourself walking to the bank after one too many unsuccessful meetings, reassess your game plan and consider whether or not your entire venture should be reworked to attract more interest.

Most likely, you'll want to look for your first investments from people you don't know, as in our scenario here. Your investments can come from an individual, more commonly called an angel investor, or an investment (venture capital) firm. Angel investors should hypothetically live up to their names; they will be less greedy because they will typically have less to offer your company. Venture capitalists (often called vulture capitalists) are normally bright, experienced businesspeople, but they will demand a lot and might not be knowledgeable of your market sector at all. They sometimes fail to realize that business models for one industry might not work as well for your company, and that one size does not fit all.

A lot of underdogs think that they can start out selling pieces of their company to their friends and family members, but there are federal regulations that complicate this process beyond what most people understand. The legal, contractual obligations required of these arrangements oblige all parties to recognize a company's ambitions as mere dreams with potentially no basis in reality. In addition, your friendly investors must certify, in writing, that they have assets above a certain level and can afford to lose everything they invest in you. The whole process is to prevent you from convincing Aunt Sally and Uncle Fred to invest their entire retirement account in your company. And once the explicit paperwork shows them that they could indeed lose it all on your venture, your once-so-enthusiastic family members might clutch their checkbooks much more tightly.

It is indeed a dog-eat-dog world. You can get money to grow any venture you wish to pursue, but the more you have thought it through and the more you have accomplished prior to your hunt for money, the better valuation you will get. After fool-proofing your innovation and assembling a first-rate company team, the world is yours to finance your success.

Chapter 10

Examining Innovation in the Workplace: Why the Underdog Isn't a Workhorse

Everyone wants innovation, but creating a work climate where innovation will thrive requires a lot more than just desire. In order to increase your company's creative capacity, you must learn to see your employees as more than just gears in your machine. Great managers are usually great psychologists; most managerial skills are actually applications of a fine knowledge of human thought and emotion, not a shrewd mind for business or lust for profit. Understand your workers as people, meet their needs, and fulfill their desires, and you will be rewarded with successes of your own.

There are several serious reasons why employees of the smallest businesses *and* the largest corporations seem to be lagging in the creativity department. The first is fairly simple to understand. As intelligent children are often bullied by their classmates and deemed bothersome by their teachers, innovative employees are often spurned by their coworkers and treated as threats by their employers. The most common complaint I hear about workers is that they are "difficult to work with." Though this criticism seems to be a euphemistic way to describe an employee who shows up late and crossword puzzles through business meetings, it is actually often a disguised way of saying, "I don't like working with that guy. He's too good at what he does and that puts pressure on me to keep up."

Many companies don't fail just because new ideas aren't being born; they perish because company managers, afraid to stray from the status quo, kill the ideas their employees do manage to come up with. Embracing novel innovations requires taking risks; unfortunately, some company heads have sat in such cushy, undemanding positions for so long that they forget how important risk-taking is to survival and success. The Wright brothers took an incredible risk when they set flight in their first, makeshift airplane. If they hadn't, none of us would have the luxury of air travel today, and the world would be a much slower, more complicated place. Risk-taking is a fundamental part of being a person, one of the purest human needs. Unfortunately, most employees are paid to do a job instead of paid to do a job *well*. Therefore, most work environments offer little incentive for workers to innovate above expectation. But a good manager knows that a high-flying employee shouldn't be cut short just to make everyone else comfortable. When a worker takes to the sky, the whole company should sail into space.

It goes without saying, then, that most company achievers are not rewarded for their innovative ideas. If employees are given incentives, they are usually only modest, superficial cash bonuses, good only for creating workplace hostility and employee resentment. Give a man a $250 cash bonus and you've simply filled his gas tank for two weeks. To discover what really celebrates a person's efforts, think about what type of acknowledgement feels best to you. Sure, extra cash is always nice, but, if you are like most people, you feel most rewarded for your work when you are purely *appreciated.* If you reward a man by giving him value and esteem, you won't just thank him for the work he's done; you will provide him the incentive to do more. Bonuses should reward past performance and stimulate future productivity. In order to do this, they must be perfectly tailored to your employees' needs.

⟋⟌

In order to inspire your employees, it is first absolutely essential to understand the hierarchy of human needs. Abraham Maslow's representation of human motivation can be seen as a blueprint for business success. His theory is illustrated in the form of a pyramid, housing five levels of human desires in order from the most basic to the most complex. They are: physiological needs, safety needs, love and belonging needs, esteem needs, and the need for self-actualization. According to Maslow, our needs follow a spectrum of satisfaction; as a person's most primal, physical desires are met, he or she will continue to seek the satisfaction of increasingly intellectual and spiritual goals. A successful business manager should create a work environment that satisfies more than just employees' basic physical and financial needs. A truly booming business utilizes reward and esteem to stimulate and maximize workers' highest needs: creativity and innovation.

Let's take a brief look at Maslow's pyramid and examine how innovation applies to all of its levels. Its lowermost level consists of our most basic physiological needs:

eating, drinking, breathing, and procreation. Activities such as eating and drinking might seem too fundamental to need help from innovation. Yet this is absolutely not true. The ancient Egyptians are excellent examples of great first-level need innovators. Finding enough food to eat isn't as simple as plucking it out of the ground; enjoying a refreshing glass of water when you're living in the middle of the desert, BC, isn't either. In order to nourish and hydrate their massive society, the Egyptians had to become expert innovators. Their plowing and irrigation systems are first-class examples of innovations in obtaining sustenance. Though today food is harvested mechanically and water is pumped through pipes, society will forever be faced with innovating food and drink. From engineering lower-calorie foods to fight the war against obesity, to using green energy to fuel food production, our world is just as dependent on first-level need innovations as ever.

The second level of Maslow's pyramid encompasses human safety needs. These range from physical safety to financial security to general health and well-being. Again the Egyptians serve as an interesting example of safety innovators. It is commonly believed that the leading causes of death in ancient Egypt were famine, warfare, and plague. But in fact, the majority of early Egyptians died from fundamental dental diseases such as abscesses. It is unlikely that the Egyptians could have innovated fluoride toothpaste to solve their mouth maladies, but, in the end, they didn't have to. It turns out that their tooth trouble could be improved significantly even thousands of years before the advent of modern dentistry. The root of the problem actually stemmed from the way the Egyptians grew their crops; because of the nature of the desert landscape, their wheat was grown in fields amid desert plains filled with sand. Therefore, lots of windblown sand was incorporated into the wheat as it was milled and processed; the end result was horribly abrasive bread. It didn't take too many years, eating sand-paper snacks before most Egyptians' teeth were worn down to the gum line or below. One of history's most life-preserving innovations seems simple in retrospect, but discovering the need to remove any sand from their wheat at harvest time was a monumental move for the ancient Egyptians.

The third level of Maslow's pyramid is the realm of social needs. These include friendship, family, and intimacy. Today's world is abounding in social innovations. With Internet technology, people can meet others with similar passions and interests all over the globe. Companionship is much easier to find in the Internet age as well; dating sites such as Match.com and Eharmony.com provide the means for singles to scan the globe for mates who match their criteria. Sites such as YouTube.com make it simple for people to share videos with family members who might live far away; similarly, software programs such as Skype have transformed the basic telephone call into a fully interactive audio *and* visual experience.

Before the very pinnacle of the pyramid (self-actualization—*aka* the realm of creative thought), is the fourth-highest category of human needs: esteem, pride, and respect. Because needs must be fulfilled from the lowliest to the loftiest, this category is the gateway to the top level of the pyramid, the ultimate human need to solve the most complex problems of the world. Because humanity's innovations have satisfied peoples' needs to eat, find shelter, maintain safety, generate families, and seek out companionship, people have reached the point at which obtaining a high level of self-esteem is the greatest driving force of their future innovations. Innovative advances that are valuable to society should undoubtedly stir up pride within their creators. But self-esteem relies even more heavily on external reinforcement. It should go without saying that innovators who benefit their fellow human beings should receive accolades for their contributions. The more innovators are praised, encouraged, and rewarded, the more apt they are to innovate solutions to ever more challenging problems. But if innovators are not properly compensated for their work, they will not reach their full potential. Worse, they will not have sufficient encouragement to keep innovating at all. Without incentive, there can be no creativity.

When a person has sufficient self-esteem, he or she will be inspired to self actualize and driven to fulfill his or her greatest potential for solving difficult problems, understanding complex morality, generating supreme creativity, and realizing great beauty. A large part of self-actualization surrounds the fulfillment of cognitive needs. Humans have an innate and overwhelming desire to learn, explore, and discover. It's no wonder that the world's most influential cognitive innovations have stemmed from history's most secure and successful societies. Once a society fulfills its people's need for food, safety, and family, once it acquires a sort of civilian esteem, its innovators are then totally free to develop the most intricate systems of language and learning as well as the most fascinating styles of art. The development of the written word in ancient China (and possibly Mesopotamia) was the initial step in an ever-outpouring flow of cognitive innovations. Through Gutenberg's printing press, beyond the age of the World Wide Web, human beings continue to constantly, cognitively innovate. And our potential for creativity only increases with the passage of time: As far back as 20 years ago, a study suggested that a person reading a single issue of the *New York Times* had access to as much information as a person living in the Middle Ages encountered in his entire lifetime.

It is unknown (and exciting to speculate about) just how far the beauty of human self-actualization will take us. People have always been capable of doing truly tremendous things with quite impeccable speed. It is almost mind-boggling to consider the evolution of human art, from the cave paintings in Lascaux to the post-modern work of Salvador Dali. It is equally astounding to regard the progression of human sound from Gregorian chants to the 12-tone music of Schoenberg and Berg. Self-actualization is what drove Archimedes to his eureka understanding of why boats float and Rodin to create his great statue *The Thinker*. It has even evolved the world of politics: Think about Ronald Regan's campaign slogan, "Are you better off now than you were four years ago?" Becoming better, faster, stronger, and smarter is what ultimately drives a person to act. In a sense, the satisfaction of physical, familial, and safety needs is not an end in itself; it is an entry to fulfilling the intellectual needs that are the true essence of humanity. Innovation is life.

❧ ❦

If you consider the critical importance of Maslow's hierarchy of human needs, you will quickly realize why current modes of employee motivation do very little to accomplish innovation. Typically, most company managers believe that they can incite more innovation with a compelling speech or two. It is quite standard practice for a manager to gather company employees together, erect a podium, and use grand, sweeping gestures, purposeful eye contact, and perfectly punctuated speech to "rally" his or her workforce to creative action. After this performance, the manager will most likely sit back and wait for innovation to happen; it is likely he or she will wait an infinitely long while.

Years ago, when people accepted jobs, they more or less accepted them for life. Everything a person accomplished was therefore mutually beneficial to the company *and* the emploee's retirement plan. Workers were the vital organs of their companies, living and growing mutually with their collective wholes. Even just 25 years ago, the average life span of a job was eight years. Today, people keep their jobs for less than five years. Mass layoffs, downsizing, rightsizing, and "voluntary" retirement—these are just some of the reasons why the average worker bounces between dozens of jobs during his or her lifetime. Such brief spans of employment cannot possibly guarantee that individual careers will grow and expand with companies. It makes little sense, then, for people to work their fingers to the bone to achieve rewards in which they will likely never share.

The ever-increasing disparity between what "big bosses" take home and what company underdogs earn is all the more reason why silly company speeches rarely spur innovation. The average salary of a CEO working for a Fortune 500 company is more than $10 million. The average salary of an employee at such a company is $38,000. These statistics are well beyond obscene, especially in light of the current financial crisis in the United States. With mortgage foreclosures forcing tens of thousands of people out of their homes, it should be immediately clear why company employees are less than enthusiastic about innovating. Elegant speech-making cannot generate creativity in the face of unfulfilled needs. Workers who aren't paid fairly will never be able to innovate; neither will those who are treated as expendable company commodities. The first step toward encouraging your employees to innovate is to take care of their financial needs. The second is to hire them (so long as they are capable and willing) for life.

But paying your people fair salaries and assigning them purposeful places in your team is not enough to stimulate their best work. You must be aware of the contributions each individual makes to your product, your service, or your business, and reward your most successful employees accordingly. Most workers are usually more afraid of suffering negative consequences than they are excited about enjoying positive rewards. It is much more common to hear, "If I don't get this assignment done, I might lose my job" than "If I go above and beyond the parameters of this particular task, I will earn the praise of my boss, inspire my colleagues, and advance my career." It is pretty easy to see that, though negative reinforcement *is* intimidating, it doesn't do much to promote good work. It's very difficult to "scare" an employee into a more resourceful, innovative frame of mind. Because innovation requires a free spirit, it will not come easily from an underdog who's been backed into a corner.

❧ ❧

Rewarding good work is similar to rewarding good behavior. There is a little-known religious order known as the Monks of New Skete in upstate New York. Part of their program of expert prayer and study includes their highly acclaimed system of training perfectly behaved puppies. Dog owners around the world consider themselves blessed to receive choice companions from the Monks of New Skete; their dogs are conditioned to be immaculately behaved members of any human family.

The puppies from New Skete are notably more loving, loyal pets than the typical trained dog because of the philosophy according to which they are raised. Most

dogs are "housebroken" according to a system of negative reinforcements. Their owners let them loose about
their houses until an inevitable accident dirties the living room carpet. Each time a dog has an accident indoors,
he is punished (oftentimes pretty severely) until he associates the act of relieving himself with the consequence
of being bopped with a rolled-up newspaper. Puppies that
are housebroken will eventually learn to control their
bodily functions well enough to make their owners happy;
they also still stand a good chance of growing into happy,
healthy dogs. Once a puppy has been screamed at repeat-
edly for making a very natural "mistake," it is unlikely
he will ever fully bond with the housebreaking humans
in his new family.

The monks, however, do not housebreak their puppies. Instead, they center their puppies' lives on frequent
and extended bathroom breaks. Every hour, on the hour,
they take the dogs outside and give them the opportunity to relieve themselves. If they do, the puppies are
effusively rewarded with praise and tasty treats. If they
do not, there are no positive rewards or negative reper-
cussions; the dogs are simply treated with the usual care
and kindness. It turns out that the monks' system of positive reinforcement for good behavior is much more
timely and efficient than the standard dog trainer's
policy of negative reinforcement. Housebroken puppies
are often very slow to learn; they spend a great deal of
time confused before they actually figure out that their
punishments are supposed to be incentives. However,
positively reinforced dogs experience so much excitement over their rewards that they are extremely eager
to learn whatever behavior is necessary to win them
more.

Most companies do not motivate their employees
through positive reinforcement. Despite all the platitudes

gushed forth by human resources organizations, employees are hardly ever rewarded for their work. Many companies maintain that positive reinforcement has little effect on company productivity and is therefore a waste of resources. In a way, they are right: The positive reinforcement systems typically used are of little value. Human "underdogs" have quite different needs than puppies; the positive reinforcements they receive must be tailored to fit their supreme need for esteem. If companies were to reward their employees *properly*, the return they'd receive in innovative capacity would be worth the world.

⊰ ⊱

So then, how is it possible to reward your people so that you make a difference in your company's productivity? You can give them cash bonuses, but you shouldn't. Once the word breaks free (and it most certainly will) about which employees received which dollar amounts as their rewards, the work environment will catch fire with resentment and jealousy. Your workers will want to know exactly what criteria you established to award the money, why so-and-so received twice the prize as such-and-such, and whether or not someone's particular brand of hard work is valued more than another's. As your employees toss evil eyes about the water cooler, each will probably take his or her money, pay a few bills, and soon forget it ever existed. Yet the resentment between your coworkers will always remain.

Whenever I observe an employee doing an especially good job at anything, my absolute first course of action is to call the local pizza shop and request two large pizzas delivered to his or her desk. Initially, it might sound crazy to suggest that a hardworking employee would enjoy even the tastiest hot pizza more than a lump of cold, hard cash. But the truth is that pizza is much more satisfying to a person's hierarchy of needs than money is. If I order two large pizzas, I have (hopefully) requested much more pie than any one human being could possibly consume in one sitting. Being unable to eat the whole order him- or herself, it is unlikely that the employee would find use for the pizza at home either; no one wins applause at the family dinner table for bringing home ice cold, partially eaten pizzas. Therefore, the natural way to address the overabundance of food is for the employee to invite coworkers to share. This is never hard to do; the smell of a terrific pizza can be detected throughout an entire office building in a matter of a few seconds. When a high-achieving hire gets to enjoy a slice of pizza with coworkers, the whole office wins a delicious way to forge stronger teamwork. You, the boss, will have only spent minimal dollars to deliver the feast. This works out to be entirely win-win for both management and staff. The former saves a huge amount from the cost of mailing out bonus checks; the latter isn't rifted by resentment. Most importantly, the pizzas provide the means for a public party, a celebration of someone's creative work. This is a prime example of how positive reinforcement can fulfill peoples' need for esteem.

Positive reinforcement is also most effective when it rewards an employee's need for family satisfaction. Most companies only see the individuals they hire, not the spouses and children attached to those people. Therefore, it is impossible for companies to consider how important family sacrifices are to employee performance. Whether they must move locations or endure long hours of separation, most families dutifully accommodate their underdogs' job as best (and often as thanklessly) as possible. If you want to keep your people working in tiptop shape, you must not only consider their needs; you must also fulfill the needs of their families.

If one of my employees' contributions was so spectacular that it surpassed the realm of pizza parties, I arranged to treat his or her entire family to a much more elaborate feast. A wonderful way to do this was to hire a beautiful, top-of-the-line limousine to take the employee and his or her spouse out for an elegant dinner. With this door-to-door service came a babysitter from a small group of child caretakers I had hired for precisely this purpose. Before the designated evening, the selected sitter would be briefed on the interests and passions of the employee's children; this way the kids would enjoy a fun-filled night and their parents could experience an evening as stress-free and romantic as possible. Because the caretakers were so carefully selected, they often hit it off with the children quite well. Sometimes they were successful to such a degree that the kids would request them as staple sitters. This meant that the parents had the incentive and peace of mind to enjoy even more nights out while the babysitters brought in more business. The whole set-up was completely beneficial to everyone involved. Again, treating an employee and his or her family to a night on the town was a much more sincerele way to thank him or her than stuffing green paper in his or her pockets.

You must remember that, as a supervisor, it's essential to understand what will get your employees "turned on" to innovation. Money is not enough; neither is a one-size-fits-all plan to boost esteem. One of your employees might find incredible joy in traveling to attend business meetings in nice locations. Another might be motivated by pure public visibility; in this case, rewarding him or her with a representative duty or the chance to present a paper might be just the right medicine for innovative health. The bottom line is that you need to provide rewards for past performance that stimulate your employees to produce at an even higher level. Remember: Your workers are your most important resources. If you take the time to understand and recognize their basic human needs, you will foster the realization of their super-human innovative capacities.

Chapter 11

Producing Creative Pups: How Parents and Teachers Can Foster Innovation in Children

Innovations always stem from at least one of three things: needs, dissatisfactions, or curiosities. However, it seems that the hallmarks of adulthood—independence, acceptance, and routine belief in the status quo—are quite the opposite of innovation's three parts. People we see as mature and self-sufficient adults may actually be dead to the notions of creative thinking and innovative change. This is because innovation is not accomplished by training one's mind to function within the rigid confines of being unimaginative and "grown up." Rather, innovative minds must run free like the minds of children. In a world full of innovators, a world that could be so exciting, comfortable, and easy to live in, children would be allowed to be children, and adults would never grow up.

Once you have trained yourself to become an innovative thinker, the creative spirit will inspire you to share your discoveries with just about everyone around you. True innovators know that the best creativity comes from collaboration. Once you've come up with some innovative ideas of your own, you will naturally want to share them with your friends, your colleagues, and especially your children. But teaching children innovation isn't quite the same as teaching them trigonometry or applied chemistry. Children shouldn't be taught innovation with the assumption that they know nothing; rather, children's natural innovative capacities should be encouraged to flourish from where they already definitely exist. Because children are natural innovators, you might find that they'll actually teach you a thing or two about innovation, things that you and I might never consider.

◆ ◆

Working with children, I am consistently impressed by how uninhibited and brilliantly capable their minds are. Throughout the years, I've been privileged to work with elementary-school-aged kids, in groups as small as 20 and as large as 150, through classes and seminars at their schools. My speeches center on innovation and illustrate how children have and can continue to become some of the world's most important creators. Any parent or teacher can utilize the structure and content of my talks to foster innovation in children of all ages.

My most recent appearances have been a part of a remarkably innovative program called Power Up Gambia. The group provides area schools with a series of educational speakers to teach students about a range of topics from innovation to economics. The proceeds from these speaking engagements are used to provide adequate electricity to a hospital in Gambia. Gambia is a nation with such a shortage of medical care and such an overabundance of illness and mortality that just a small increase in power is enough to save thousands of its people's lives.

I've found that kids get just as (if not more) excited about an assembly on innovation as they would about a trip to the zoo. Added to their excitement is the joy of many Gambian children now able to receive critical surgery because their hospital's lights will be lit for one more day. And so, as a whole, Power Up Gambia is an innovation in itself because, at the same time that it cares for the minds of children on one side of the world, it cares for the bodies of children living on the other. Hopefully, the type of innovative thinking taught by Power Up Gambia will only continue to snowball in its significance. I like to think that, when these kids grow up, their problem-solving capacities will have wiped out sickness in Gambia so that its children can also focus on nourishing their minds instead of salvaging their bodies.

This can only happen if the kind of energy generated at the Power Up Gambia seminars is spread throughout elementary and high schools all across the United States. The seminars are simple enough to replicate because they don't depend on elaborate skill or knowledge; in fact, a lot of the questions I ask the kids to explore have answers that are not related to any branch of science at all. All it takes to teach children innovation is a little bit of imagination and some creative fun.

❧ ❧

I begin all of my children's seminars by explaining the three sources of innovation: needs, dissatisfactions, and curiosities. Knowing that innovation doesn't stem from algebra, chemistry, or an extensive knowledge of Latin is usually a great relief to kids who are happy to acknowledge that they indeed have a lot to be needy, dissatisfied, andcurious about. Sometimes, however, these terms need a little bit of clarification. For example, usually when I first ask kids to tell me about some of their needs, they tell me they absolutely need things such as Xbox 360 and Nintendo Wii. I usually use these examples of "needs" as a platform to explain the differences between a need and a want, the latter usually being a synonym for dissatisfaction and not a requisite for life.

Ironically, a lot of times, kids understand the difference between a need and a want even more quickly than most adults. (How many of us are at all times ready to swear up and down that we absolutely need that new plasma screen TV while things such as doctor checkups are routinely pushed to the far reaches of our to-do lists?) When I ask kids to tell me about some of their needs a second time, they usually get much closer to the mark by suggesting things including food, shelter, and medicine.

Once, a little boy in the audience told me that his neighbor's dog often tried to bite him and that his greatest need was to figure out a way to get the dog to stop. The rest of the kids and I agreed that safety is definitely one of human beings' inherent needs. At first thought, the solution to protecting this little underdog from the nasty canine's bite seemed pretty simple; immediately many of his classmates suggested that all he needed to do was talk to his neighbor about the problem. Yet it turned out that the dog actually belonged the neighbor's teenaged son, a much-less-amicable character. Moreover, the solution to the dog-biting problem required some special attention to the young man's integrity; even though the boy was getting quite scared of the dog, he didn't want to look cowardly by asking for help from his parents or neighbors instead of solving the problem himself. I'm not sure where he found the courage to bring the issue up in front of his friends and classmates, but I am awfully glad he did.

As the kids brainstormed other possible solutions, everyone agreed that hurting the dog was not an option and that trying to scare the dog would be counterproductive; barking back at the mutt or throwing things at him would only agitate him further and might prompt him to charge at the boy *Sandlot* style. The more we talked about the problem, the more the students became excited by the opportunity to "save" one of their classmates and the more the ideas started spilling out of their eager mouths. A lot of their suggestions were certainly creative; one student suggested that the boy get a pet tiger and take it for walks by the neighbor's house. Another boy tried to apply what he knew about his own dog's fear of lightning and suggested that the boy carry a camera around with him so he could scare the dog with the flash.

Though these suggestions were all very much in touch with the imaginative component of innovation, they were far away from innovation's practical side. Ultimately we decided that the best thing to do was condition the dog to associate attacking the boy with something unpleasant. Once we decided on the type of action to take, figuring out the specific course was a cinch; all we needed was a young lifetime's amount of experience. I reminded the children that a huge part of innovating a solution to any problem is being able to take what you know from one part of life and apply it to another. Therefore, in order to find the magic ingredient unpleasant enough to make the dog stop, we only had to look at what kinds of things the students themselves found disagreeable.

The kids immediately started chattering away about all the things they didn't enjoy. Most of the kids noted how too much homework and striking out at baseball made them sad. But dogs don't get homework and they don't play baseball, so we all agreed that we couldn't use homework or baseball to improve this particular dog's behavior. Then one little girl mentioned she had gotten soap in her mouth in the shower that morning, and the fact that she could still taste it made her very unhappy. At first the other students seemed irritated that the little girl would even think to compare her soapy mouth to something as serious as a bad homework assignment or an embarrassing baseball game.

But then another student realized the value of her suggestion and took the idea one step further. He announced that the solution to the dog problem was simply to carry around a squirt gun filled with soapy water (or something equally noxious). This way, every time the dog lunged at the little boy, ready to bite him, the boy could just squirt the soapy water into the dog's mouth where the obnoxious taste would linger for hours. The little boy was delighted with his classmates' suggestion, and he was so proud to have thought through the problem with his peers instead of complaining to his parents.

The next time I made a trip back to that school, the little boy was very excited to report that he had tried the soapy squirt gun solution and it had worked fabulously. The first squirt had temporarily stopped the dog dead in his tracks, and, just four episodes later, the dog had been successfully conditioned to stay 8 feet away. Inspired by his own ability to solve problems, the boy then came up with the idea to upgrade his gun to a farther-squirting model with more power. This did the job of keeping the dog 20 feet away, and after so many uses all the boy had to do was put his hands on his hips to keep the unruly pup in line. In addition to making his walk to school a lot more peaceful, this solution has also allowed the boy to have a much better time once he gets there; I understand from his teacher that he has gained quite a lot of stature among his peers because he didn't confess he was scared of the dog to adults.

❧ ❧

The next part of my children's seminars involves working with the students to develop innovative solutions to life's dissatisfactions. I like to pitch the kids this question: "Other than your siblings, your parents, and your school, what annoys you the most?" I find the answers are usually beautifully diverse. They range from restricted television and video game time to being forced to eat requisite food groups to having to suffer through school dances. Regardless of the specific grievances I collect at any given seminar, kids' complaints are usually best addressed by social or process innovations (innovations needed to overcome obstacles related to other people or procedures). Children's greatest adversaries (at least in their own minds) are their parents; this means that the solutions to virtually all of their problems involve the earning of privileges, the negotiation of alternatives, and the attainment of substitutes.

A girl once presented the problem she had with her parents constantly nagging her to clean her room. Upon expressing the problem, she received some sympathetic feedback from the rest of her classmates, validation that her troubles were widely felt among her peers. She then proposed a solution consisting of some very interesting storage cabinets with drawers that would automatically retract into invisibility whenever she pushed a button. I was pretty impressed by her classmates' critical assessment of this idea; they collectively pointed out that, though the storage drawers would quickly conceal the girl's mess, they offered no innovative way for her to more quickly or efficiently move the mess from the floor to the drawers in the first place.

At this, the girl put forth another solution: a disposable roll of plastic that would cover the carpet and retract on command with her messy floor's contents in tow. This idea was a much better solution; in fact, a similar process is already being put to use: Retractable/rotating plastic "sanitary" devices are being "received" quite well on select toilet seats across the country. It seems as though the idea could prove to be the new frontier in cleaning up all sorts of messes. Marketing the idea could be a problem, though; the system installation would require adult permission and adult income, but the point here is that a small child can come up with a rather remarkable grown-up idea in a relatively short amount of time with just the right amount of discussion. This is because children are dissatisfied just as much as (and often because of) adults.

❧ ❧

The third and final source of innovation is curiosity, and, when I talk to kids, I often save this concept for last. I find that out of all three, curiosity is the origin of innovation that gets kids excited the most. This is because contemplating curiosity is an extremely positive and limitless experience. Innovating out of curiosity versus needs and dissatisfactions means not being restricted to thinking within any negative confines or parameters. If you're not thinking about the things you don't have and/or don't like, you are much more likely to reach for what you could have and/or love. It's easiest to get kids to think creatively because children don't like to think about all of the boring things they need and all of the frustrating things they don't like. Adults, however, have the most difficult time innovating out of curiosity; their lives revolve around making sure their needs are met and their dissatisfactions are managed.

I start the creativity segments of my elementary innovation workshops by asking what sounds like a silly, curious question: "Where does the phrase 'happy as a clam' come from?" Initially most of the kids laugh because they think they can't possibly understand what cheerful marine life has to do with the science of innovation. But they are all eager to agree that the saying doesn't make any sense. Once we agree that the statement deserves an explanation, I go on to explain that the only time I ever get up close and personal with a clam, I am about to eat him (or her). Therefore, if clams are intelligent, they should only be terrified, hence unhappy, every time they come into contact with human beings. If clams are not intelligent, then the concept of being happy versus unhappy would never cross their minds, and they wouldn't be capable of experiencing either emotion. Therefore, it could be concluded that human beings have never actually seen a happy clam, regardless of whether or not clams are intelligent. Because "happy as a clam" cannot possibly reference real joyfulness, the phrase must have been inspired by some instinctual or intentional clam behavior people perceive as happiness.

The notion of happy clams is usually enough to relax the kids into a fun frame of mind so that they always have a ton of suggestions about the origin of the idea. One boy challenged the belief that intelligent clams would not be happy to be eaten; he insisted that sitting in water with nothing to do but eat micro-particles of food all day was so boring that a clam doing any such thing would jump at the chance to be turned into a delightful culinary creation. Another child decided to completely overturn my proposition that the happiness or unhappiness of a clam is solely dependant on whether or not it is to be eaten; she claimed (in more words or less) that the fact that clams don't have to do homework makes them so happy that their bliss blinds them to the finality of death.

This question about cheerful crustaceans sounds silly on the surface—almost as silly as the answers it receives. But the aim of asking this question is neither fun nor foolishness; the purpose of this simple exploration is to allow children to think critically about things they take for granted (how many of us use figures of speech without having any idea where they come from?) and to challenge the way authority says we should approach a problem. (It could very well be that clams' emotions are wired so differently from humans that death makes them quite happy instead of sad.)

❧ ❧

Children are too often trapped into the nasty cycle of intellectual regurgitation. This mode of teaching children limits them to learning about what people have discovered in the past. But children don't learn everything from this; opening up a child's innovative capacity means giving him or her a sense of empowerment. So many educators and even politicians try to win us over with slogans such as "children are our future." They neglect to consider that the only link to the future is the present, and that preparing the next generation to take on the world means including them in what's going on right now. Children are surprisingly able to take on some serious problems facing the world. For example, global warming, a problem adults haven't even collectively acknowledged, can only be tackled by a generation of innovators consistently prepared to think about solutions from the start.

Most of the kids I've worked with have heard about global warming, but they have no idea what it is or how serious its implications could be. A lot of young people don't understand why a 5-degree increase in temperature is such a big deal; consequently they might start to believe that global warming is a small issue that some adults have exaggerated into a large problem. This is dangerous, because what young people should be learning about the global warming crisis is that it is in fact *more* frightening than even most of their parents think.

Though global warming is a complex problem, it is easily broken down to be simply and interestingly explained to children. When I lecture to students, I first explain the importance of temperature to wind currents and the importance of wind currents to the growth of crops. Illustrating to the kids what a slight change in temperature could do to our weather and our food supply is easily done by reminding them of their history book's lessons about how most wars have been fought over land and food. When children hear this, it is absolutely incredible to see how quickly the lights go on in their heads as they realize that they have been cheated out of knowing all of the ramifications of warming. They had thought that (worst case) people would have to wear short-sleeved shirts instead of long sleeves in the spring and the fall.

Kids don't need to feel daunted by such a problem as global warming, because learning about what caused the issue can be quite interesting. For instance, most kids don't know about the role that the dairy industry plays in global warming. But they become immediately interested and highly entertained when they learn that the methane gas produced by dairy cows is so present and so potent that it is 50 times more damaging as a greenhouse gas than even carbon dioxide. The kids usually get a huge laugh when (inevitably) at least one member of the class suggests that global warming could be solved by putting hoses at the rear ends of all the world's dairy cows and capturing their flatulence as a source of renewable energy. And so they are quite disappointed when I explain to them that 90 percent of that methane gas comes out a cow's mouth instead of its other end; they find it hard to imagine all of the world's cows eating with gas masks over their faces.

The point to all this discussion is that kids are very easily turned on to the idea of innovation. Engaging them to talk about their fears, their dissatisfactions, and their tremendous amount of curiosities is such a simple yet powerful way to light a fire in their minds. The most important thing I have learned from my exchanges with children is that they are constantly opening my mind up to new ways of seeing things I had never even considered before; maybe clams *are* happy they don't have homework! Kids have a priceless perspective, and their creativity isn't just something cute in the classroom; children can be brilliant innovators in the business world, too.

❧ ❧

The fact of the matter is that children have been innovating throughout history, just as long as adults have. About 150 years ago, a 15-year-old grammar school dropout named Chester Greenwood invented earmuffs to protect his ears from windburn as he ice-skated. He actually patented the idea and established the Greenwood Ear Protection Factory in Maine (which is now the earmuff capital of the world). More recently, a young lady from

Massachusetts named Kathryn Gregory invented Wristies, accessories designed to form a barrier between glove tops and coat sleeves, in order to protect people's wrists from snowy seepage. Kathryn's idea was so appealing that she was able to sell her innovation through Girl Scouts, McDonalds, and even the home shopping network QVC.

One of the greatest childhood innovation stories I've come across is that of My Little Footsteps, tiny adhesive "right" and "left" shoe labels designed to help kids put their sneakers on the correct feet. For centuries, children have been made to feel inadequate and unintelligent for not being able to put their shoes on correctly; yet no adult has ever thought of a way to make the task easier. Some parents think that finding a temporary solution to the shoe situation could harm children by giving them permission to avoid learning the difference between right and left. In a way, they are right, because thinking *for* children can be a dangerous thing. But allowing children to innovate a creative prosthesis to help them bridge the gap between confusion and clarity is not only the best way to help them survive childhood; it is the best way to prep them for a successful adulthood.

Six-year-old Christopher was just like any other kid; he was altogether unable to match the subtle curves of his shoe soles to the opposite shapes of his right and left feet. One day, after his mother pointed out his mismatched shoes for what seemed to be the thousandth time, Christopher got frustrated and exclaimed, "Gee Mommy; you'd think that grownups would have invented something to help us kids put our shoes on the right feet!" Christopher's mother was shocked at her son's rather brilliant exclamation, and instead of further chastising him for his mistake, she encouraged him to go one step further with his dissatisfaction.

In the fashion in which my mentors would have guided me, Christopher's mother generated questions and gave him the right tools to help make his idea a tangible reality. She asked him what he thought could help him sort out his shoe problem. Immediately Christopher exclaimed that putting pictures of his feet on his shoes would be the best way to solve his problem. The two took out an assortment of arts and crafts supplies, and almost instantly little Christopher was inspired to dip his feet in paint and stamp out his prints on cardboard. Those templates became the first prototype for My Little Footsteps, an incredibly innovative and nationally selling product.

A lot of parents wouldn't even consider helping their children to market their ideas; in a world where getting kids off to school in the morning is a significant challenge, introducing them to the world of product marketing might seem nearly impossible. But in actuality, kids make much better businesspeople than students because working in the business world allows them to be actively involved in what is going on around them. Though he required a lot of adult help, Christopher was extremely involved in the entire process needed to walk his footsteps into the homes of thousands of children across the nation.

Through very simple research, Christopher's mother determined there was nothing on the marketplace that resembled her son's proposition; he had tapped into and found an exclusive solution to a problem suffered by almost every small child in the world. With utmost faith in his creation, little Christopher and his mother met with a patent lawyer to do a search of existing patents. After filling out the provided paperwork, Christopher became one of the youngest patent holders in the country. Next, they trademarked a product name and procured an artist to develop the picture to be put on the labels.

At this point in the process, Christopher and his mother had to start thinking carefully about the finer points of his product. They needed to create a label that could endure the sweat of a child's sneaker and the wear and tear of washing machines while meeting FDA approval as a nontoxic product. They needed to determine the size of the label, meet with glue manufactures to find the right materials, find a manufacturer, discover a packager, and acquire a UPC code. All of this required a lot of adult insight, but Christopher's childlike charm was the most crucial part of selling a successful product.

Because underdogs work best with other underdogs, Christopher and his mother targeted their sales pitch to all of the small, independent shoe retailers in their area. Christopher would personally walk his product into each store and give the owners his pitch. This plan was perfect, because time after time Christopher would leave the stores a very satisfied salesman, exclaiming, "Mom, they liked my labels!"

Eventually, the product was receiving orders from all over the United States, and Christopher started garnering publicity for his idea. Local papers and then national publications such as *USA Today* began running stories on the 6-year-old innovation wiz. Christopher appeared on the *Today* show and CBS Business's *This Morning* show. My Little Footsteps grew so big that it found a home in places little Christopher could have never imagined; the young entrepreneur eventually received a call from the head of an orthotics center, where the product was helping children put their braces on the right legs. With this news, Christopher and his crew went back to the drawing board to design smaller, stickier labels produced on bulk rolls so that the product could be sold in large quantities to orthothic centers across America.

❖❖

Here is the bottom line when it comes to teaching children to innovate: Children are the ultimate underdogs. And the biggest barrier between the underdog and its innovative capacity is the crushing force of authority. The fact is that underdogs are intimidating; they have the most needs and the most dissatisfactions, and this makes them perfectly primed for innovation. This is something the people in charge know and are desperately fighting against. This relationship between innovative underdogs and overbearing overlords is unfortunately quite analogous to the relationship between kids and many of their parents and teachers. Too many adults have grown too used to discouraging kids' complaints because such dissention makes grownups feel undermined, defensive, and disrespected. If we really want to promote a future full of innovation, we must sincerely listen to young people in the present. This will make everyone's lives a whole lot easier. We sure won't have to worry about putting the right shoes on the right feet.

Chapter 12

Seeing Green: How the Underdog Innovates a Cleaner, Richer World

Underdogs are purebred to love the news. Today, underdogs can access up-to-date, cutting-edge information from all over the globe in ways that are much more delightful than just bringing in the daily paper. Now, to fetch his daily fix of facts, an underdog must only hop on the computer and nudge the mouse about with its nose before opening up a world of information and innovation inspiration. If ever an underdog feels its creativity lagging or its level of curiosity sagging, all it needs to do is refocus its priorities on its imminent needs. In order to be fiscally successful, a person must plan ahead for his or her current funds to address the forthcoming concerns. Similarly, and all too importantly, the people who comprise a successful planet must be able to use the present to innovate an extended and flourishing future.

Just because you have your bases covered today doesn't mean you'll have no problems securing them 10 years from now. And the issues you think you can ignore until the far-off future might be much more pressing than you currently care to acknowledge. For years, news headlines have been screaming with scary statistics about environmental devastation; however, people's knowledge of this problem has done little to initiate any innovative solutions. Society is extremely concerned with innovating new and improved products and novel elements of culture; these creations provide the short-term satisfaction many people (especially Americans) adore. However, humans have not been as interested in creating ways to reduce the pollution those innovations generate or lower the levels of energy they consume. Now though, it is becoming ever more clear that people must stop abusing the environment if they want to remain on this planet. Therefore, the future of humanity depends on a future rich with innovations that solve age-old problems such as environmental destruction, nonrenewable energy, and global warming.

Most underdogs will agree that the world's most pressing concerns are obvious; of course, global warming, world hunger, widespread infectious disease, and transcontinental energy crises are all terrible trials that must be dealt with. But interestingly, though the world's greatest issues are at the forefront of everyone's thoughts, no one has yet come up with any real groundbreaking solution to any one of these concerns. It is tempting to believe that the greatest problems of the world remain unsolved because the question "how can it be done?" remains unanswered. However, the real question to ask is not "how can these problems be solved?" but "who is going to solve them?"

There might have been a time when all the underdogs of the world could rest assured that the bigwigs in power would somehow find a way to mend every hole in the universe. However, it is now fairly apparent that this is not the case. Because the people in charge are so preoccupied with trying to make a dollar, they have remained completely ignorant of the environmentally damaging consequences of their actions. Furthermore, the people at the top of the economic pyramid have no desire to help the health and wellness of those at the bottom. For that reason, ancient maladies such as malaria continue to ravage the vast majority of the planet. Now, it is no longer okay for the underdog to leave innovation up to the overlord; the latter will never see the world's most serious situations solved. This chapter is designed to take a comprehensive look at our planet's major issues in order to help the underdog put parameters on the problems and consider them carefully for solutions.

❧ ❧

Let's take a look at the situation caused by global warming. Many sets of statistics are floating around that report (according to one organization or another) just how much the earth is warming due to our heavy use of fossil fuels and our overproduction of greenhouse gases. However, though the facts and figures vary a bit among environmental studies, there is no doubt that the numbers indicate a disturbing trend that must be dealt with sooner versus later. Credible sources predict that the Earth's climate will suffer catastrophic changes with each and every degree its average temperature is amplified. If our planet sees just a 6-degree increase to its normal climate, the swell will be great enough to bring humankind to the brink of extinction (assuming that wars resulting from inadequate food supplies don't destroy us first). What can be done to innovate our way out of such a grim, premature fate?

There are two particularly promising ways in which innovations for energy consumption can begin to heal the planet. The first is perhaps the most obvious: We should all try to use less energy. There are many ways that individual underdogs can cut their consumption of fossil fuels; for instance, they can better insulate their houses and drive more fuel-efficient cars. However, unless the entire planet comes together in a massive conservation effort, the global climate won't change much at all. Conservation is a spectacular thing, and it certainly aids in the effort to keep our temperatures down and our earth clean, but there are several reasons why conservation cannot be counted on to singly save the planet.

First of all, it is highly unlikely that all the people belonging to all the countries of the world will converge on a mutual conservation policy. Too many nations depend on foreign oil sales to generate domestic revenue. Furthermore, the effort to conserve is contradictory to the human desire to make money; too much of our economy is driven by usage (not the avoidance of use) for conservation to be embraced by all. It is nearly impossible to make money by conserving anything, especially the energy everything runs on. Unless innovators devise an extremely creative way to profit off of conservation, the funds to promote and deploy such a policy will never be available.

The second set of potential solutions requires that we use more eco-friendly types of energy instead of burning fossil fuels. A cursory examination suggests that we actually have lots of alternative sources of renewable energy available to us that are generally efficient and friendly to our atmosphere. Solar, wind, and geothermal energies are all unconventional, yet much cleaner sources for powering our homes, our cars, and even entire cities. Biofuels extracted from plant waste and even

184

our own garbage have also been proposed as a possible clean energy option. Why is it, then, that none of these suggested solutions have taken center stage to reverse the world's energy and environmental crises? The answer is that, although most alternative energy sources look good on paper, they are crippled with complications that make them easier spoken of than applied. Hydroelectric and geothermal energies are indeed creative alternatives to oil, but they might not be as out of the box, and therefore successful, as other energy innovations human beings have yet to come up with.

❧ ❧

Hydroelectricity has received much hype recently as the ultimate source of renewable energy. It is quite true that hydroelectricity possesses distinct advantages to fossil fuels. First and foremost, hydroelectricity is much more economically friendly than conventional energy sources; hydroelectric plants do not require fuel, and, because they are automated, they have little to no operational costs. Hydroelectric plants are also, in part, more ecologically sound; they do not directly produce carbon dioxide, a common fuel-firing plant emission and a potent greenhouse gas. Yet, hydroelectricity owns almost as many negatives as positives. The main concern associated with hydroelectric plants is their negative impact on air and aquatic life. Hydroelectric plants alter both water currents and water temperatures in such a serious way that many types of fish and the birds that eat them are becoming endangered. Hydroelectric dams are also responsible for completely changing the planet's geography.

Consider the Three Gorges Dam in China: It produces a great deal of electricity, but it is also drowning numerous important archaeological sites through silt buildups that cause rising water levels and landslides.

Hydroelectric dams, such as the Three Gorges Dam, are also not as innocent of creating greenhouse gas emissions as they might have once seemed. It has recently been shown that hydroelectric dams are responsible for creating significant quantities of methane and carbon dioxide. This is because plants decaying in areas flooded by the hydroelectric dams actually produce large amounts of greenhouse gases as they decompose. Considering all the facts, though hydroelectricity is almost certainly more beneficial than burning fossil fuels, it seems it is only just a step in the right direction when it comes to innovating a truly efficient mode of global power.

Geothermal power, which is energy harvested from heat stored beneath the Earth's surface, in its atmosphere, and under its seas, is also touted as a promising energy substitute. Indeed, geothermal energy has worked well in countries, such as Iceland, where the Earth's heat is stored relatively close to its surface. However, throughout the vast majority of the planet, the Earth's energy is not nearly as cheap or as easy to access. The deeper one must drill to acquire the Earth's heat source, the more expensive that energy becomes to acquire. Consequently, geothermal energy constitutes less than 1 percent of the world's energy supply. Furthermore, it is highly unlikely that human beings will ever extract enough renewable heat energy from the planet's core to change its climate one iota (even in the next several thousand years). Recently there has even been some doubt raised regarding whether or not geothermal energy is truly a renewable energy source at all. Some geothermal sites have reportedly even "cooled down"; this news could indicate that geothermal energy can be irreversibly depleted. Because geothermal energy could ultimately prove unreliable, and because it presently proves difficult to harvest, it looks as though this form of power doesn't quite fit the bill for world-wide energy reform either.

❧ ❧

Biofuels are yet another example of energy that looks good on paper—until one computes its impact on our land and our bodies. Just because a material is a natural, carbon-based substance doesn't mean it cannot become harmful once you burn it. Studies have shown that biofuel consumption emits dangerous levels of formaldehyde, a well-known cancer-causing agent. Levels of atmospheric formaldehyde and similar carcinogenic substances are reportedly more than 100 to 200 percent greater in countries that consume biofuels than in those that utilize traditional fossil fuels. Additionally, the deforestation undertaken to grow biofuel crops is displacing and endangering animals, and even tribes of indigenous people. Finally, pesticide use has been significantly increased by biofuel crop cultivation. Consequently, clean water supplies are suffering in locations where biofuel use is increasing. Clearly, biofuels are not such bio-friendly alternatives to fossil fuels.

❧ ❧

There are also several ways that human beings can harvest energy naturally from the sky. Wind turbines generate energy as air currents spin their aerial blades; the kinetic energy accumulated by the turbines can then be transformed into other, more useful kinds of power. Though wind turbines work very well to generate energy, they can only be operated according to the whims of the world. Man has not yet discovered a way to manipulate weather patterns; until he does, wind turbines are only as powerful as the wind that blows through them. Unfortunately, wind power is not as strong or consistent as human beings' need to produce eco-friendly energy. Wind turbines have also earned themselves reputations as "poultry processers" because their rotating blades often assault flying fowl. Even if the wind turbines do manage to miss chopping up an entire flock, migratory birds are rightfully frightened by the giant structures, and therefore forced to abandon their normal migratory patterns. This can greatly endanger bird species and drastically affect all the members of the food chain (including humans).

Solar energy is perhaps the most promising alternative energy source contrived thus far. It seems simple and logical enough that people should easily be able to harvest a massive amount of energy from the brightest star in our sky. After all, there are copious amounts of solar energy striking the Earth's surface each day. However, there are many problems associated with solar power that prevent it from becoming our primary energy source any time soon. Like wind, sunlight does not always occur when and where we want it. Additionally, the technology required to capture and convert the sun's energy is, relatively, very expensive. Perhaps the biggest disadvantage of solar energy is that it cannot be captured at night. Therefore, innovators must devise a way to store solar energy so that excess energy captured during beautifully sunny days can be used when the sun sets or the clouds come out. As far as one can predict, this technology is entirely possible, and the field presents many wonderful opportunities to the world of innovation.

You don't have to possess an advanced science degree to consider solving the global energy crisis. Even if you do not own the technical know-how or academic expertise necessary to put a solution to practice, you are still capable of exploring the parameters of the problem in order to come up with a unique set of answers. You might think that the average underdog is under-qualified to solve a problem such as "how to store solar energy." Yet it is very possible for any person possessing even the most rudimentary scientific knowledge to conceptualize innovative solutions to the toughest problems. For instance, perhaps innovating a more efficient way to use solar power has little to do with the complicated mechanics behind storing energy and everything to do with the knowledge of simple states of matter. Perhaps solar energy needn't be stored at all; a truly novel approach to the problem might suggest that how solar energy is put to use matters more than how frequently it can be captured. What if solar power was used to freeze water during the day? Then the ice could provide air conditioning during the night as it reverted back to its original liquid state.

❧ ❧

It is quite possible that the solution to the planet's energy crisis has nothing to do with any of the alternative energy sources mentioned here. It could be that innovating a successful new mode of power requires innovators to approach the problem from an entirely different avenue. Sometimes, just to get your creative juices flowing, it helps to conjure up a truly audacious solution to the problem at hand. You never know what creative gems you might unearth with just a little courageous thinking. Considering solutions that might seem whacky or far too out of the box might prove beneficial to finding a logical, workable solution; this is because using your wildest imagination frees up your entire brain to analyze any problem. Even if your eccentric solution has zero chance of working, it should serve as a fun and satisfying springboard for finding creative ideas with just a little more potential.

Consider, for instance, how the electric eel could inspire a new innovative power source capable of preserving the planet. Electric eels generate enough electricity to completely stun most living creatures. And their ability to shock the living daylights out of their prey might just inspire a way for human beings to keep the lights on in their houses without destroying the Earth. An electric eel generates its power by utilizing a bunch of tiny biological batteries it charges as it goes about its business. When an eel decides to attack, it simultaneously latches on to its victim with both its mouth and its tail, completing a circuit and successfully shocking the organism. Though electric eel energy probably won't become the world's next power source, the science behind their capabilities is certainly significant enough to be successfully applied to other biological energy generators.

Suppose that people innovated a way to install electric eel-like batteries inside green plants. Plants are already such spectacular sources of electrons because they undergo photosynthesis, the process by which a plant converts sunlight into fuel. What if people were able to capture plant life's bountiful electron stores? Photosynthetic electrons could be siphoned off through copper wire and then stored in biological batteries implanted in either genetically engineered plants or those injected with conductive nanoparticles. Then people could use that energy to completely change the course of human civilization. This redirected plant energy could allow us to purify our water, enable our communication, drive our cars, heat our houses, and a whole lot more without any capital expense and no environmental damage. Could such a solution work? Possibly; possibly not. However, the notion is deserving enough to be pursued more seriously. The idea is also valuable because it exemplifies the thought process behind truly creative ideas.

⚔ ⚔

The possibilities for innovation in energy efficiency are endless. You might even discover an innovative way to use power while attempting to solve a completely different problem. For instance, I absolutely hate to have pizzas delivered. It seems to make no difference from which business I order a pizza, or what time of the day I try to have it delivered; every pie I have ever received has arrived cold, soggy, or both. Some companies have tried to address this problem by delivering their pizzas in nice, insulated carry boxes. However, though these devices might maintain the pizzas at an edible temperature, they do nothing to preserve their texture and flavor. A pizza insulated in a thermal carry case is just about as enjoyable as leftovers. In order for a slice to be truly delectable, it must be consumed piping hot from the oven as soon as it's reached its peak color and consistency. How could the entire delivery process be upgraded to transport top-quality pizzas from the restaurant to the customer's house every time?

If one considers all the resources available to the delivery driver, one will quickly discover the potential hidden in his or her car's engine. An automobile's engine creates a great deal of heat, which otherwise flows freely out of its tailpipe. What if, instead of wastefully expelling the delivery car's heat into the atmosphere, pizza-delivery restaurants decided to utilize that heat to cook their pies en route to their customers? With just a little thought and basic engineering, pizza entrepreneurs could construct heat exchangers in their delivery cars; the system would attach to the engine block in order to superheat a closed-loop liquid system running through to a passenger-seat pizza oven. (The heating system would be sealed, of course, protecting the bubbling pizza from exposure to exhaust fumes.) This innovation would make it possible for the pizza restaurant to prepare the pizza on location while postponing its trip to the oven until minutes before it reaches the customers' door. The pizza would then be delivered at its freshest and most delicious. Furthermore, by utilizing heat already generated by delivery cars instead of running huge in-store pizza ovens, the pizza restaurant could save itself and the environment the expense of extra fuel consumption. Who knew that innovating a way to deliver fresher pizza could work to improve the planet?

❧ ❧

Regardless of your background, your job, or your education, you are more than capable of considering how to solve the world's most severe environmental problems. You only have to understand the nature of innovation and its key components. Part of what fuels innovation is the proverbial saying that "one man's meat is another man's poison." Think about the waste humans generate, waste that litters the earth and pollutes the water. Quite a number of years ago some varieties of bacteria were specially modified to eat oil from spills. These specially engineered organisms work relatively well—so well that they have aided in treating messes such as that of Exxon Valdez. Precisely how the bacteria are able to eradicate the oil is not completely understood, but the basic principles are pretty simple.

If one thinks about how to solve new problems by modifying solutions to similar problems, one might suggest that people could create bacteria capable of cleaning up other hazardous materials and diseases from our water. Perhaps people could go even one step further and produce bacteria that could eat sand to manufacture electricity. Though these ideas might seem far-fetched, they are indeed entirely plausible. Consider the world's geothermal vents, cracks in the Earth's surface located deep down in its oceans. These cracks often release large quantities of hot water that's loaded with sulfur and other minerals. Even though there is no sunlight and virtually no oxygen within these vents, they are still a suitable home to some unusual plants and animals. One type of vent-dwelling organism is a rare breed of bacteria that lives off of sulfur and thrives in hot, acidic water. Even more remarkable, this kind of bacteria changes and mutates hundreds of times more quickly than bacteria residing above water.

What if we could "repurpose" this type of bacteria in order to eat humankind's wastes? Perhaps it could be adapted to eat the exhaust from power-generating facilities that burn fossil fuels or the sulfur that makes acid rain. There are infinite opportunities associated with such fascinating organisms. All that the innovative mind must do to seize these opportunities is think as one would in a Chinese restaurant: Take one element from column A, apply it to a problem in column in B, and you stand a good chance at discovering a groundbreaking innovation.

Chapter 13

Innovating the Impossible: How the Underdog Moves Mountains

Throughout the history of humankind there have been three major revolutions. The Agricultural Revolution saw society split into two new groups: the urban and the rural, the latter growing the food the former consumed. Later, the Industrial Revolution witnessed the steam engine and other technologies become levers to human muscle, enabling bigger and more complicated structures to be built more quickly and with more efficiency. Today, we are living in the Information Revolution, the age in which computers are projected to perfect human intellectual function in the same way the tools of the Industrial Revolution improved man's physical capacity. Many people believe that computers will soon become more than just cognitive prostheses and calculators; some even predict that computers will eventually surpass and take over the functions of the human mind, fulfilling the ultimate sci-fi scenario. But is this really possible?

It is true that much of what society has science-fictionalized in mainstream media has become, or has the potential to become, reality. Take, for instance, the technology projected by the Spielberg sci-fi film *Minority Report* based on the short story by Philip K. Dick. In this movie, Tom Cruise stars as John Anderton, the chief of Washington D.C.'s division of the futuristic, elite crime fighting force, "Precrime." This system utilizes three genetically superior humans, "Pre-Cogs," who are able to see the crimes of the future and thus convict criminals, "pre-crime," in the present. Much of the film's magic stems from Cruise's all-star manipulation of Precrime's Biometric Security System, technology that regulates Internet and computer database access by voice, fingerprint, iris, and retinal scans. Spielberg set biometrics halfway into the 21st century, but, interestingly enough, it looks as though his estimate was extremely cautious; scientists predict that biometric technology will take society's center stage as early as 2010. Very soon, people will be able to use their own bodies as passwords to access their computers, cell phones, and even their own front doors.

❧ ❧

Sci-fi movies reflect more than just the inspiration behind technological innovations such as biometrics. They also predict additions to the realm of social innovations. When *The Truman Show* was released in 1998, people marveled at the film's seemingly far-fetched subject: a suburban man who discovers his life is actually a television show, his neighborhood is a sound stage, his friends and family members are actors, and none of his experiences have been "real." At first, this film seemed only fun fantasy; it was thought that a world where people's lives are broadcast on public television could only exist in the realm of social fiction. However, just a short time after *The Truman Show* met cinematic success, reality television became all the rage on the small screen; a barrage of shows from *Big Brother* to *Survivor* to *The Simple Life* found smashing success exploiting "real" people doing "real" things in "real" time.

Following these examples, it might make sense to assume that all science fiction will eventually meet serious reality. But this isn't the case. Take the Terminator movies as fine examples of sci-fi not likely to see fruition. Most people would agree that the time travel inherent to the movies' plots will never exist. Yet the Terminator films' central subject, artificial intelligence (evolved beyond human control), is a concept many people fear. It is important to note that, although many of the futuristic innovations we see in Blockbuster hits are promising additions to our future, not all of Hollywood's high-tech ideas are viable. The supreme example of an impossible innovation is an artificial intelligence that surpasses and conquers humanity. Though they may compute complex figures more quickly and accurately, provide the means for lightning-speed communication, and now host touch-screen technology that makes it possible to manipulate graphics as solid objects, computers will forever lack the most important component of intelligence: the ability to innovate.

But all human beings are capable of innovating infinitely, and not just in the social and technological worlds of the future. One might believe that the only way to innovate today is within the realm of the computer and communication technology of the Information Age. However, there is still plenty of room for new innovations in industry and agriculture. For instance, once, it seemed okay for society to produce its food by drowning the world in pesticides; in the past, people simply didn't

197

know how harmful pesticides can be to the body and the environment. Now, as civilization moves toward what is known as the "Green" Revolution, people are (slowly) recognizing the importance of innovating better ways to nourish the world.

There are many other troubling areas of society that are routinely overlooked, yet still clearly in need of some innovative first aid. For instance, until Hurricane Katrina hit, people believed that the Corps of Engineers could fix any flood disaster. The devastation that still haunts Louisiana today proves that even existing systems might need some major renovations before they actually work. Just because a domain is old does not mean it has no need for innovation. If Hollywood sci-fi films have taught us one thing, it is that human beings are capable of innovating an "impossible" future. This chapter should teach you that we are also capable of innovating the "impossible" problems of the past and present. Innovation truly transcends time; new technology and/or new ways of thinking can solve even the most ancient of problems.

❧ ☙

My students often need some gentle reminding that creative thought can change even the oldest, most primal aspects of the human experience. Therefore, I often assign exercises that challenge my college-age students to innovate age-old activities. Once, during a particularly entertaining lesson, I asked my classroom to come up with creative ways to innovate sex. I explained that sex is probably the oldest of all human activities; if sex can be innovated with modern technology, just about anything can. As soon as these words left my mouth, I saw a series of jaws drop like dominoes across rows and rows of desks. Many of my students laughed out loud; some openly questioned my sanity. Still others didn't understand the purpose of the assignment at all; they couldn't see why something that's functioned fine for thousands of years would ever need a boost from modern know-how. A lot of pencils hit the floor that day; a lot of thumbs twiddled about in the air. Yet, one of the guys in the classroom took the exercise seriously—and came up with a brilliant idea.

The next week that student walked into class with a fully thought-out, prototyped solution to a common sexual conundrum. As he sat down in his seat, he proudly presented me with the first rough model of his innovative idea: a pair of sports cardiovascular monitoring systems. The gadgets consisted of sensors that strap across athletes' chests and wrist receivers that indicate vital stats such as pulse and heart rate. As I listened to him explain his idea, I could gauge that the young man had expertly followed all the steps of the innovative process. First, he carefully identified a problem that has plagued love-makers since the beginning of time: the inability to detect (definitively) whether or not one's partner's bedroom enthusiasm is sincere. Next, he fully assessed what his solution had to achieve. Using a basic knowledge of human biology, he acknowledged the correlation between external sexual response and internal changes such as accelerated heart rate. Then he assessed the world around him for other activities that depend heavily on heart rate.

Being a young man, he naturally thought about athletic training. Next, he applied existing sports monitoring technology to his particular problem; taking heart rate monitors from the treadmill to the sheets, he decided that clearly visible statistics were the best way to encourage bedside honesty. His solution proposed that each partner strap on the monitoring chest sensors and swap the corresponding wrist monitors; this way, each

199

person could note changes in the other's pulse and heart rate. Without having to make any real modifications to the technology of the monitors, the young man packaged them up and began selling them across campus as the novel new sex toy named "No Faking." His brilliance in both applied technology and marketing made him a lot of money that school year.

In order to discover innovation's full and lasting potential, one has to constantly reassess problems previously thought to be impossible. The young man in my innovation classroom was able to sell a great quantity of No Faking devices to college students of all ages and both genders. Considering his success, it is obvious that his innovation addresses a fairly universal problem. It is interesting to consider why the situation hadn't been solved before. It could be that the issue was too intimate for the average person to acknowledge and assess. Perhaps it was too low on peoples' lists of priorities for them to pay too much attention to. Whatever the reason, the No Faking innovation illustrates some of the most important human attributes a successful innovator should consider. First, people are reluctant to solve their personal problems, *but* they will pay almost any amount of money for someone else to do the dirty work. Similarly, an innovator always has opportunities to solve the problems people are too busy or stressed out to get to. A lot of times, "impossible" problems are only those that are either embarrassing or stuck at the bottom of the list.

❧ ❧

Many problems only seem impossible because we've thought of them as such for so long. Some "impossible" problems have even become proverbial, such as that notion that "one cannot move mountains." But both new technologies and new ways of thinking can make it possible to prescribe new solutions to even prehistoric problems. When it comes to landscape shifting, you'd be surprised how efficiently modern know-how can accomplish some of the most monumental tasks. If you follow the principals of innovation—asking questions, defining the problem, and searching everywhere for the solution—almost anything is possible. Learning to "move mountains" in the 21st century should not be a Herculean task. In my classroom, it's just a standard part of the college curriculum.

One seemingly ordinary day, my students took their seats, opened their notebooks, and assumed expectant yet peaceful postures. They were anticipating that I would lead a relatively average discussion that day, but, boy, were they wrong. As soon as they uncapped their pens, I passed out a sheet of paper: a pop quiz. The standard, collective grumble ensued, but the noise died down suddenly as the kids read the assignment before them. Each piece of paper contained five concisely written tasks:

1. Eliminate all causes of global warming in 30 days.
2. Send a man to the moon for $5 or less.
3. Build a working time machine.
4. Move the Rocky Mountains.
5. Raise a billion dollars by lunchtime tomorrow.

I advised that they all work quickly; I expected the quizzes to be completed within 30 minutes. Of course the classroom erupted with commotion as the students began working furiously on their assignments. Brains were on fire and ears were steaming as pencils scribbled notes and calculations across each test sheet. By the time

30 minutes were up, half the class looked cross at their shredded papers; half were sprawled across their desks in defeat. Before they had a chance to protest, I scooped up all of their papers, crumpled them together, and tossed them swiftly into the wastebasket. At this point, the class was outraged, so I conceded to tell them why I threw their answers away. My explanation was simple: No one, not one student, bothered to ask a single question about the parameters of the assignment. They all assumed that I had fully and completely defined the problems and memorized a full and comprehensive enumeration of all the possible "trick" or "hypothetical" answers. Most importantly, they all felt defeated by how "impossible" the problems seemed. But if I had assigned questions that were just as difficult, yet less out of the box, the class would have felt confident asking as many questions as were allowed.

Some of my students looked quite sheepish; others looked acutely stunned. After a minute or so, one young lady timidly raised her hand and asked me if I would kindly explain the parameters of the problems. Others joined in this very sincere effort to redeem themselves, but I decided I would first direct the discussion toward a scenario that really could be impossible. My purpose was to show my students that questions, not first impressions, are what yield information about a situation's possibility.

I asked the class to consider the time machine. I challenged them to conjure up several reasons why a person would like to own and operate such a device. At this point, most of the group seemed too nervous over whether they should answer my question or pose questions of their own. So I helped them along. I proposed that I myself would love to travel back through time to the beginning of the last century. I happened to know where to snatch up the best first-growth Bordeaux wines of that time, easily and inexpensively, as real "liquid assets." To show them I was serious about this scenario, I offered a post-class wine and cheese party to the entire group—if only one of them could prove my proposition possible or impossible.

As thoughts of slivered fancy cheese and fine red wine began to bubble about their brains, I saw a switch go off in the faces before me; they were starting to get the idea. After a few minutes, one young man vigorously raised his hand and confidently questioned how I could expect the wine to age appropriately when my lightning-fast time travels would deny it the opportunity to reach its full flavor. Of course, his question was sharp; he was absolutely right. Our discussion then progressed to the question of how I could hide the wine through the course of history, in a place where it would be exposed to the proper environmental conditions (while escaping discovery) until I was ready to deliver it in the present. After we discussed a few possible ways the wine might age in secret, another student raised one more expert question. He wanted to know how the wine would actually be paid for. Our current currency would be of no value to the businessmen of the past. Another student suggested that barter might work; however, this suggestion was soon also deemed unfit—time travelers from the future would have no identity in the past. Entering into a legally binding contract before you have (technically) even been born is impossible.

After we spent considerable time talking about time travel, it became clear that my fine wine scheme was legally, financially, and metaphysically impossible. However, if none of my students had asked questions or raised objections, it is likely they would have tried to work out the problem for hours in vain. Whether a problem seems likely to attract a solution, or nearly impossible to solve, the only way to classify the situation is by asking questions— lots of them. Even if you discover that a particular problem can be solved, things are almost never as straightforward as they seem.

Satisfied with what the class had learned, I then brought the conversation back to the original set of questions I had assigned. I decided to have everyone work on solving problem number four: transplanting the Rocky Mountains. This time around, the class was prepared not to jump the gun. Before they even thought about possible solutions, they raised their hands with a bundle of questions. One young lady was particularly wise; she knew that *why* I wanted to move the Rocky Mountains was just as important as the fact that I wanted to move them at all. I rewarded her question with a very specific answer. I told her (hypothetically of course) that I had always dreamed of building a house in Colorado; however, I would never invest in such a project until the location gained a view of the Pacific Ocean. The class was greatly relieved that my desire to move mountains was only to improve my personal view of the West Coast. If I, for instance, wanted to move the Rockies in order to build houses on its land, the situation would have been quite unsolvable. In order to pave the way for level development, the class would have had to engineer a massive geophysical project requiring several hundred years, tens of trillions of dollars, and the complete, cataclysmic upheaval of North American weather patterns. By asking one simple question, however, my students were able to transform their assignment from an impossible, senseless task, to a very manageable mission.

Shortly after they determined their objective, the entire classroom was abuzz with thought. Eventually, they came up with a brilliant, innovative solution to my mountain problem, one that didn't require me to *physically* move the Rocky Mountains at all. Instead of installing west-facing windows in my Colorado dream house, the class suggested that I put up giant flat-panel television screens in each room and feed them live Webcam footage from the Pacific. I was thrilled with their suggestion and, as they packed up their things at the end of the class, I let everyone know they would receive an A for the day's work. One student earned herself an A-plus. Before everyone left, a usually quiet young lady raised her hand to tell me that she had figured out how to solve problem number five. It was entirely possible for her to raise a billion dollars in a day, she said; all she had to do was "marry it." With that exceptional suggestion, class was dismissed.

We were able to discover solutions to two out of five "impossible" problems that day, just by learning how to ask comprehensive questions and creatively use resources. See if you are able to determine whether or not the other three problems are possible to solve. I bet, after finishing this chapter, you will have all the inspired know-how you will ever need to accomplish such a task.

❧ ❧

Great innovators are truly very resourceful; they don't consider any problem impossible until they've tried to solve it with all of the tools they have. As with all great skills, resourcefulness is acquired through much practice and brain training. By the time most people reach adulthood, the world has trained them to think rigidly about solving problems; if the answer isn't immediately obvious or the tools aren't readily available, people tend to think they've run out of options. We all have the established ways of the world so ingrained in our brains that our limited thought patterns are often hard to break free from. However, the more you understand the way you think, the more you will be able to change it.

It takes a lot of "rewiring" to open up the innovative part of your mind. One of the brain's biggest shortcomings is its tendency to consider the superficial circumstances around the information it receives more than the information itself. There was a truly classic experiment that illustrated this phenomenon brilliantly; it showed that how humans think is a direct correlation to how information is presented to them. The study's setup was simple enough. Researchers obtained a 3-foot-long metal tube with an opening slightly larger than a ping-pong ball. They welded a flat plate to the bottom and fixed the tube, open side up, to the floor. They then dropped a solitary ping-pong ball down the tube and invited their subjects into the laboratory to try and fish it out.

The first group entered a room containing nothing but the ball in its tube, a skein of string, a roll of sticky tape, a vacuum cleaner, a pitcher full of water, and a stack of paper cups. Many of the subjects tried (in vain) to extract the ball with a loop of tape attached to a length of string. However, this methodology didn't work for a variety of reasons. To start, it was essentially impossible to coax the string down to the ball; the tape at the end of the string would constantly stick to the sides of the tube before it even made it halfway down. In the very few cases in which the string was able to reach the bottom, there was no way to put enough pressure on the tape in order to adhere it to the ball. Eventually, the subjects gave up on the string and tape and generated a plan B.

Soon after, they tried to stick the hose of the vacuum cleaner down the tube in order to suck the ping-pong ball out. Unfortunately, the diameter of the hose was too large to fit inside the tube. Frustrated, the subjects tried blowing the exhaust air from the cleaner across the top of the tube, with the hope that this would generate enough suction to lift the ball out by sheer aerodynamics. This, obviously, did not work. Thinking they had run out of options, and frustrated at their lack of progress, the subjects poured themselves glasses of ice-cold water and sulked.

When a second group was brought in, the scientists kept almost all of the experiment's variables the same: The ball in the tube, the string, the tape, and the vacuum cleaner were all still inside the room. However, the pitcher of water and the paper cups were absent; in their place was a bucket full of dirty water, shoved in the corner as if left by the laboratory's janitor. Though the subjects still attempted to fish the ball out by sticking the tape to the string and suctioning the tube with the vacuum cleaner, they quickly figured out that the answer to their problem was to simply flood the pipe with water and float the ping-pong ball out. Although both groups had easy access to this solution, the way the water was presented to each group determined whether or not the subjects viewed it as a tool or a refreshing beverage.

This experiment presents all future innovators with an extremely important moral: When a problem seems impossible, take a second look at the materials you have at hand. Chances are you've failed to maximize your arsenal by overlooking all the different ways in which your tools can be used. No problem should be abandoned until you've considered each of your materials in a multitude of ways.

❧ ❧

There's not much in this world that's impossible. Even the science-fiction material of most Hollywood hits is not all that far-fetched. Likewise, "impossible" problems of the past become more possible each day as new technologies and ideas help generate more creative ways to search for solutions. You are capable of solving age-old aggravations and realizing fantastic, futuristic technologies. All you have to do is ask questions and creatively manipulate your materials.

Afterword

You have a lot to learn about innovation. First, you must understand how all innovations spring from three sources: needs, dissatisfactions, and curiosities. As you seek to fulfill your needs, overcome your dissatisfactions, and satisfy your curiosities, you must learn to ask critical questions and define solvable problems. Most importantly, you must also be able to look outside yourself and your situation for unique and even unlikely solutions. We've all heard that great innovators "think outside of the box," but what exactly does this mean?

Thinking outside of the box is about breaking down the boundaries your life has built up in your brain. Chances are good that the world around you has trained you to approach problems with certain assumptions about their solutions. For instance, one might think that the cure for intolerable pain could only be found in synthetic drugs created in pharmaceutical labs. However, one true innovator discovered that the world's most powerful painkiller resides in the venom of a tiny snail. Sometimes, the best solutions aren't obvious, even in hindsight; instead, their discoveries require incredible creativity and unrivaled flexibility. The absolute heart of innovation is the innovator's ability to use one unlike scenario as a template for solving another.

Most people are not accustomed to seeking out and considering obscure solutions. In fact, for some, thinking out of the box might (at first) seem downright painful. But training one's mind to think a certain way is analogous to training one's body to excel at a particular sport. By using special equipment to exercise your brain, you'll soon find that your mind is both strong enough to support a wealth of information and flexible enough to expand in all different directions.

❧ ❧

Throughout the years, I've devised many exercises for the purpose of keeping my innovative mind fit. The one I find works best is actually a simple way to overcome the brain's tendency to separate different classes of information. For example, the part of the brain that ponders pain and the part that thinks of wildlife are kept relatively isolated from each other; therefore, considering a new pain-killing drug hardly ever conjures up thoughts of snails. Some innovators are so extraordinary that their brains can make terrific leaps with little resistance. For the rest of us underdogs, simple office supplies are enough to unite the radically different parts of our complex minds.

If you want to become more creative, go to your local stationery store and purchase a package (or two) of 3 × 5 index cards. While you are at it, pick up a few large rubber bands (about the size you used to make slingshots when you were young). Wrap a rubber band around each stack of note cards, and keep one set with you in your purse or your pocket as you go about all parts of your day—working, running errands, even just spending time with your kids. Each time you encounter something that intrigues you, irritates you, or inspires you, write it down on a separate note card. Do not attempt to categorize what you write down, include indexing terms, or write any additional information besides the fact or the problem itself.

This exercise might seem trivial, but a surefire way to spark your creative brain is to periodically work with the information you have accumulated (in this case, on your cards). Every once in a while, take them out and shuffle them; this might become difficult once you have garnered thousands of cards, but, believe me, the struggle is well worth it. Once your hands have combined all the cards, deal them out in pairs. Look at each pair carefully and try to see if the random juxtaposition of any two items gives you any insight. Employing note cards to partner two thoughts you experienced on two separate occasions is using what I like to call a "thought prosthesis"—a tool that enables your brain to bend in ways it otherwise could not.

The reasons this thought prosthesis works are both simple and complicated at the same time. The note cards' most basic function is jogging an innovator's memory by helping him or her retain and recall information he or she encounters in day-to-day life. One of the biggest and simplest hurdles for an aspiring innovator to jump over is the inability to remember what he *or she would* innovate if he or she could. By writing down your needs, dissatisfactions, and curiosities, you are solidifying your desires and acknowledging your individual need to innovate.

❧ ❧

This thought prosthesis also tackles some of the more complicated problems our brains encounter while trying to think creatively. For instance, one of the hardest things for the innovative mind to overcome is its struggle to utilize old information. Studies have shown that the more time has passed since a person learned or thought about a particular piece of information, the farther that information exists from his or her mind's realm of intellectual comfort. Put simply, lessons we learned long ago are harder to remember. In this way, the mind works similar to the universe: According to the Big Bang Theory, the structure of the universe is ever expanding. Furthermore, the farther matter is located from the center of the universe, the faster it is traveling. Similarly, the farther information is from our present-day experience, the more quickly it will escape our grasp entirely. By writing down your thoughts on note cards, you will not only retain ideas that would otherwise leave your mind, but you will also be able to assess those old ideas in the company of new ones. The combination of both new and old ideas is one of the most fantastic recipes for innovation.

Thought prostheses are also excellent methods for combating the information overload that can prevent our minds from innovating. A lot of times, when it comes to innovation, too much information can be just as bad as not enough. It can be difficult for our brains to prioritize and sort through all the information we are exposed to in just one day. To understand this concept of information overload, it is helpful to compare all the bits of information in your brain to all of the books in your local bookstore. Have you ever gone to your favorite Barnes and Noble in search of a good book, only to find nothing interesting among the many shelves and tables? A hundred years ago, when books were commodities, most people were extremely interested to read just about anything they could get their hands on. Today, we have access to a gigantic selection of books published on almost every subject imaginable; yet it seems as though we have to hunt through them all to find something we deem "worth reading." Why is it that the more options we have, the more time we spend trying to find something good?

The reason is that, with so many books competing for our attention, it is hard to pick just one to read at a time. Psychologists have demonstrated that our inability to think clearly in the midst of information overload is a physiologically consistent behavior. In one study, scientists took human subjects and surrounded them with increasingly loud and complicated auditory stimuli. They found that people can ignore ambient distractions—to a point. Eventually though, we reach a spot where we have absorbed all we can and are thus incapable of processing any more noise. From this point forward, our ability to perform cognitive tasks actually decreases as our brains expend more and more energy just to fight off all the stimuli. By keeping your ideas on a collection of note cards (instead of letting them flounder around in your mind), you will be able to physically restrain all of your thoughts and ideas. By selecting random note cards to consider together, you will be able to unite two unlike ideas that might otherwise forever swirl around separately on opposite sides of your brain.

Keeping a stack of note cards with your past and present concerns and fascinations is also a wonderful way to keep your innovative ideas up to date. For instance, remember the student from Chapter 13 who combined an age-old universal frustration with modern sports-monitoring technology in order to revolutionize intimacy? What if all he had to do to come up with this concept was juxtapose a note card containing a common complaint with one holding his curiosity about the applications of personal monitoring systems? What if, further down the road, he utilizes an idea written on a new note card to improve his already existing innovation? Perhaps he will come to be fascinated with Apple's iPhone and decide to integrate its touch-screen technology into a new and improved model of No Faking. Remember that innovation is not just a single task; it is an everlasting process. Good ideas are always up for revisions, and a true innovator knows that his or her work is always in progress. Keeping your mind fresh with cognitive prostheses is a wonderful way to establish creative longevity.

⋈ ⋊

There is a wonderful little anecdote that perfectly illustrates one of the greatest challenges facing innovators: the task of taking on innovation as a way of life. It goes something like this: Once, there was a little boy who was terribly excited to start kindergarten. The night before the first day of school, he laid out all his clothes, checked to see that his pencil box was well stocked, and made sure he had a broad spectrum of colored paper to go along with his new pair of scissors (and a spare pair in case they broke). On the morning of the big day, he awakened before dawn and roused his sleeping parents at 4:30 a.m. For hours before the school bus arrived, he checked and rechecked his backpack and endlessly examined himself in the mirror. When the bus (finally!) came to pick him up, he darted for it gleefully before his mother even had a chance to say goodbye.

At the end of the day, the little boy's mother met him at the bus stop and asked him about his day. Joyfully, he replied, "Mom, it was wonderful, fabulous; it really rocked!" The next morning, his mother went into his bedroom to awaken the boy for his second day at school. Somewhat groggy, the little boy protested, "Mom, why are you waking me up?" When she explained to him that it was time to go to school, the little boy retorted, "What—again?"

Learning about other people's innovative achievements can be incredibly exciting and energizing, but this isn't enough to light a creative fire in your own life. You, the underdog, now possess the tools you need to generate your own successful innovations. Do not rest on you laurels; go forth and innovate!

Acknowledgments

David Pensak

First off, I want to thank my tireless publicist and friend, Karen Ammond, president of KBC Media (kbcmedia.com). Since the first time we met she encouraged me to write this book. Without her support and introductions to Bill Gladstone and Elizabeth Licorish, this book would still be just a dream, never to be realized.

Next, I want to thank my literary agent Bill Gladstone. He believed in me as well as the premise of this book. His talent as an agent is truly one-of-a-kind.

To say that I am most grateful to Michael Pye and all the folks at Career Press would be an understatement. Thank you for publishing this book and believing in this project.

Next, I must pay tribute to my wife Karen and my son Jacob. They paid a dear price for all the time I spent completely absorbed in the content of this book.

Finally, I would like to thank my co-author, Elizabeth Licorish, who is truly the only writer who could have written *Innovation for Underdogs*. Her brilliance in writing and creative thinking breathed life into my stories.

As you will read and understand, this book is dedicated to my father, who tried valiantly to teach me how to be a creative scientist. My successes are to his credit. I take the blame for all the failings.

Elizabeth Licorish

I would like to extend my warmest thanks to the wonderful people at Career Press. It was extremely rewarding to produce this book with such a fantastic team.

Many thanks to Karen Ammond, for her unwavering dedication to *Innovation for Underdogs*. Her passion and enthusiasm for this project were truly infectious.

I especially want to thank Bill Gladstone for his untiring work in seeing this project through to publication.

Of course, I must thank David Pensak for the influence of his incredible freethinking.

I am most grateful to my mother, Debbie Licorish, for teaching me how to tell a story. I am so very fortunate to have learned from the wisest, wittiest woman I know.

Finally, my deepest gratitude is owed to Christopher Barrett, who truly possesses the patience of a saint. For the endless encouragement, consolation, and three-hour book-chats over Wegmans' sesame chicken, I can never thank him enough.

Index

About the Authors

David Pensak

Dr. David Pensak, PhD, is one of the country's most prolific and successful innovators. A critical force in research at DuPont for 30 years, Dr. Pensak also founded Raptor Systems, the computer security company that developed and brought to market the first commercially successful Internet firewall. He has 38 patents and applications being prepared in fields ranging from agricultural chemistry to solid state physics to business process modeling. Dr. Pensak is highly esteemed both domestically and internationally; he has taught at the world's most prestigious universities and lectured at its most powerful corporations. Currently, Dr. Pensak is launching his International Innovation Center.

Elizabeth Licorish

Elizabeth Licorish is head writer for KBC Media, a media relations firm. She has worked with many high-profile clients, including international business moguls, TV producers, actors, and artists. She writes a film review column and has authored numerous political and social commentaries. Her work will be featured in an upcoming title from the *Chicken Soup for the Soul* series. *Innovation for Underdogs* is her debut book. She writes from her home in New Jersey.